SCHAUM'S
OUTLINE OF

Theory and Problems of
SOFTWARE
ENGINEERING

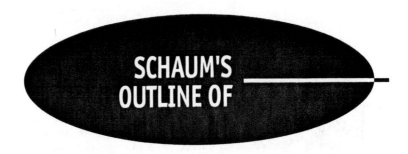

SCHAUM'S
OUTLINE OF

Theory and Problems of

SOFTWARE ENGINEERING

DAVID A. GUSTAFSON

Computing and Information Sciences Department
Kansas State University

Schaum's Outline Series

McGRAW-HILL

New York   Chicago   San Francisco   Lisbon   London   Madrid   Mexico City
Milan   New Delhi   San Juan   Seoul   Singapore   Sydney   Toronto

Dedicated to Karen, Jill, Joel, Steven, Michael, Brooke, Kristin, Matthew, Jarod, Callie, and Eric

DAVID A. GUSTAFSON, Ph.D., has degrees in Mathematics, Meteorology and Computer Science. He earned a PhD in Computer Science from University of Wisconsin, Madison. He is a professor in the Computing and Information Sciences department at Kansas State University. He has taught software engineering for over 25 years at both the undergraduate and graduate levels. His research interests include software metrics, software testing, software maintenance and robotics. He is the author of over 30 conference and journal papers and has contributed articles on software testing and software metrics to engineering encyclopedias. He has contributed chapters to books on software metrics and software maintenance. He coauthored a textbook on compiler construction. His robotics teams have participated in many robotics competitions, including a first place finish in the AAAI 1997 "Find the Remote" competition. For over 15 years, he has reviewed software engineering standards as part of the IEEE Standards Association. He is a member of Tau Beta Pi, IEEE, IEEE-SA, ACM and AAAI.

Schaum's Outline of Theory and Problems of
Software Engineering

7 8 9 10 11 12 13 14 15 16 17 18 19 20   DIG/DIG   0 9

ISBN 0-07-137794-8

Sponsoring Editor: Barbara Gilson
Production Supervisor: Elizabeth J. Shannon
Editing Supervisor: Maureen B. Walker
Compositor: Keyword Publishing Services

Library of Congress Cataloging-in-Publication Data applied for.

McGraw-Hill

A Division of The McGraw-Hill Companies

Theory and Problems of
SOFTWARE
ENGINEERING

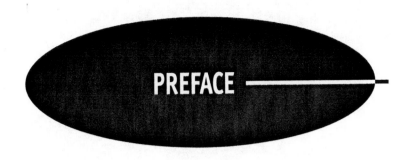

PREFACE

Software Engineering is not just surveys of techniques and terminology; it includes techniques that students must master. This book is designed for college students taking courses in software engineering at the undergraduate and graduate level. During my 25+ years of teaching software engineering at both the undergraduate and graduate level, I have realized the need for solved examples and for guidance to help students with these techniques.

This book is intended to be used in conjunction with a textbook or lecture notes on software engineering. The background and motivation for diagrams, notations and techniques are not included. Included are rules about proper construction of diagrams. Instructions on using techniques are given. Rules are included about applying techniques. Most important, examples and solved problems are given for diagrams, notations, and techniques.

Writing this book was not a solitary effort. Many people have influenced this book. In particular, I wish to acknowledge the following: Karen, my wonderful wife, for all of her support and help in creating this book. Without her help, this book would not have been done. Steve, who took time from his PhD studies to critique many of the chapters. My students, who provided the original inspiration for writing this material and who have read these chapters as individual readings, have found mistakes, and have offered suggestions. I would like to thank Ramon, who suggested this book, and the McGraw-Hill editorial staff for their help and suggestions.

DAVID A. GUSTAFSON

CONTENTS

CONTENTS

CHAPTER 1

The Software Life Cycle

1.1 Introduction

The software life cycle is the sequence of different activities that take place during software development. There are also different deliverables produced. Although *deliverables* can be agreements or evaluations, normally deliverables are objects, such as source code or user manuals. Usually, the activities and deliverables are closely related. *Milestones* are events that can be used for telling the status of the project. For example, the event of completing the user manual could be a milestone. For management purposes, milestones are essential because completion of milestones allow, the manager to assess the progress of the software development.

1.1.1 TYPES OF SOFTWARE LIFE CYCLE ACTIVITIES

1.1.1.1 **Feasibility**—Determining if the proposed development is worthwhile.
Market analysis—Determining if there is a potential market for this product.

1.1.1.2 **Requirements**—Determining what functionality the software should contain.
Requirement elicitation—Obtaining the requirements from the user.
Domain analysis—Determining what tasks and structures are common to this problem.

1.1.1.3 **Project planning**—Determining how to develop the software.
Cost analysis—Determining cost estimates.
Scheduling—Building a schedule for the development.
Software quality assurance—Determining activities that will help ensure quality of the product.

Work-breakdown structure—Determining the subtasks necessary to develop the product.

1.1.1.4 **Design**—Determining how the software should provide the functionality.
Architectural design—Designing the structure of the system.
Interface design—Specifying the interfaces between the parts of the system.
Detailed design—Designing the algorithms for the individual parts.

1.1.1.5 **Implementation**—Building the software.

1.1.1.6 **Testing**—Executing the software with data to help ensure that the software works correctly.
Unit testing—Testing by the original developer.
Integration testing—Testing during the integration of the software.
System testing—Testing the software in an environment that matches the operational environment.
Alpha testing—Testing by the customer at the developer's site.
Beta testing—Testing by the customer at the customer's site.
Acceptance testing—Testing to satisfy the purchaser.
Regression testing—Saving tests from the previous version to ensure that the new version retains the previous capabilities.

1.1.1.7 **Delivery**—Providing the customer with an effective software solution.
Installation—Making the software available at the customer's operational site.
Training—Teaching the users to use the software.
Help desk—Answering questions of the user.

1.1.1.8 **Maintenance**—Updating and improving the software to ensure continued usefulness.

1.1.2 TYPICAL DOCUMENTS

1.1.2.1 **Statement of work**—Preliminary description of desired capabilities, often produced by the user.

1.1.2.2 **Software requirements specification**—Describes what the finished software will do.
Object model—Shows main objects/classes.

Use case scenarios—Show sequences of possible behaviors from the user's viewpoint.

1.1.2.3 **Project schedule**—Describes the order of tasks and estimates of time and effort necessary.

1.1.2.4 **Software test plan**—Describes how the software will be tested to ensure proper behavior.
Acceptance tests—Tests designated by the customer to determine acceptability of the system.

1.1.2.5 **Software design**—Describes the structure of the software.
Architectural design—The high-level structure with the interconnections.
Detailed design—The design of low-level modules or objects.

1.1.2.6 **Software quality assurance plan (SQA plan)**—Describes the activities that will be done to ensure quality.

1.1.2.7 **User manual**—Describes how to use the finished software.

1.1.2.8 **Source code**—The actual product code.

1.1.2.9 **Test report**—Describes what tests were done and how the system behaved.

1.1.2.10 **Defect report**—Describes dissatisfaction of the customer with specific behavior of the system; usually, these are software failures or errors.

1.2   Software Life Cycle Models

The four different software life cycle models presented in the following sections are the most common software life cycle models.

1.2.1 THE LINEAR SEQUENTIAL MODEL

This model, shown in Fig. 1-1, is also called the waterfall model, since the typical diagram looks like a series of cascades. First described by Royce in 1970, it was the first realization of a standard sequence of tasks.

There are many versions of the waterfall model. Although the specific development tasks will occur in almost every development, there are many ways to divide them into phases. Note that in this version of the waterfall, the project planning

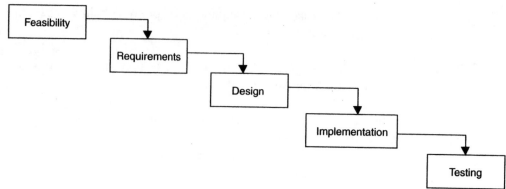

Fig. 1-1.   Waterfall model.

activities are included in the requirements phase. Similarly, the delivery and main-tenance phases have been left off.

1.2.2   THE PROTOTYPING MODEL

This software life cycle model builds a throwaway version (or prototype). This prototype is intended to test concepts and the requirements. The prototype will be used to demonstrate the proposed behavior to the customers. After agreement from the customer, then the software development usually follows the same phases as the linear sequential model. The effort spent on the prototype usually pays for itself by not developing unnecessary features.

1.2.3   INCREMENTAL MODEL

D. L. Parnas proposed the incremental model.[1] The goal was to design and deliver to the customer a minimal subset of the whole system that was still a useful system. The process will continue to iterate through the whole life cycle with additional minimal increments. The advantages include giving the customer a working system early and working increments.

1.2.4   BOEHM'S SPIRAL MODEL

B. Boehm introduced the spiral model.[2] The image of the model is a spiral that starts in the middle and continually revisits the basic tasks of customer com-munication, planning, risk analysis, engineering, construction and release, and customer evaluation.

---

[1] D. Parnas. "Designing Software for Ease of Extension and Contraction." *IEEE Transactions on Software Engineering (TOSE)* 5:3, March 1979, 128–138.

[2] B. Boehm.. "A Spiral Model for Software Development and Enhancement." *IEEE Computer.* 21:5, May 1988, 61–72.

Review Questions

1. How does a phased life cycle model assist software management?

2. What are two required characteristics of a milestone?

3. For each of the following documents, indicate in which phase(s) of the software life cycle it is produced: final user manual, architectural design, SQA plan, module specification, source code, statement of work, test plan, preliminary user manual, detailed design, cost estimate, project plan, test report, documentation.

4. Order the following tasks in terms of the waterfall model: acceptance testing, project planning, unit testing, requirements review, cost estimating, high-level design, market analysis, low-level design, systems testing, design review, implementation, requirement specification.

5. Draw a diagram that represents an iterative life cycle model.

Answers to Review Questions

1. How does a phased life cycle model assist software management?

The phased life cycle improves the visibility of the project. The project can be managed by using the phases as milestones. More detailed phases will allow closer monitoring of progress.

2. What are the two required characteristics of a milestone?

A milestone (1) must be related to progress in the software development and (2) must be obvious when it has been accomplished.

3. Documents in the software life cycle:

Final user manual	Implementation phase
Architectural design	Design phase
SQA plan	Project planning phase
Module specification	Design phase
Source code	Implementation phase
Statement of work	Feasibility phase
Test plan	Requirements phase
Preliminary user manual	Requirements phase
Detailed design	Design phase
Cost estimate	Project planning phase
Project plan	Project planning phase

Test report   Testing phase
Documentation   Implementation phase

4. Order of tasks:

Market analysis
Project planning, cost estimating, requirement specification (may be done concurrently)
Requirements review
High-level design
Low-level design
Design review
Implementation
Unit testing
Systems testing
Acceptance testing

5. Draw a diagram that represents an iterative life cycle model. See Fig. 1-2.

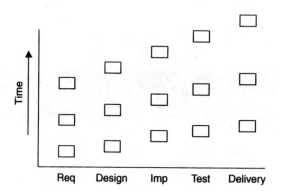

Fig. 1-2.   Iterative life cycle model.

CHAPTER 2

Software Process and Other Models

2.1 The Software Process Model

A *software process model* (SPM) describes the processes that are done to achieve software development. A software process model usually includes the following:

- Tasks
- Artifacts (files, data, etc.)
- Actors
- Decisions (optional)

The notations used can vary. The standard software process model uses ovals for tasks and processes. The artifacts are represented by rectangles and the actors by stick figures. Many software process models do not include decisions. We will use diamonds whenever we show decisions. The flow is shown by arcs and is usually left-to-right and top-down. Arcs are normally not labeled.

The following are rules and interpretations for correct process models:

- Two tasks cannot be connected by an arc. Tasks must be separated by artifacts.
- A task is not executable until its input artifacts exist.
- There are one or more start tasks and one or more terminal tasks.
- All tasks must be reachable from the start task.
- There is a path from every task to the terminal task.

Software process models can be *descriptive*; that is, they can describe what has happened in a development project. The descriptive model is often created as part of a postmortem analysis of a project. This can be useful in terms of identifying problems in the software development process. Or, software process models can be *prescriptive*; that is, the software process model can describe what is supposed to happen. Prescriptive software process models can be used to describe the standard software development process. These can be used as training tools for new hires, for reference for uncommon occurrences, and for documenting what is supposed to be happening.

EXAMPLE 2.1

Figure 2-1 is a process model for unit testing software. There are two actors: the tester and the team leader. The unit tester, of course, is responsible for the unit testing. The unit tester uses the source code and the test plan to accomplish the unit testing. The result of this activity is an artifact, the test results. The team leader reviews the test results, and the result of this activity should be the approval of the unit testing. This model does not explicitly show what happens when the process is not successful. It could be inferred that the unit tester keeps testing until he or she is happy. Similarly, if the team leader is not ready to give the approval, then the process may be backed up to redo the unit testing.

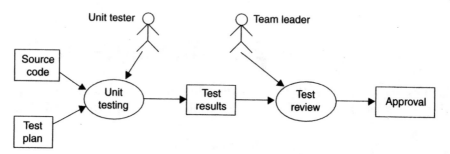

Fig. 2-1. Process diagram for unit testing.

EXAMPLE 2.2

Draw the process model showing decisions.

Adding decisions allows the process model to be more explicit about what happens in all circumstances, as shown in Fig. 2-2.

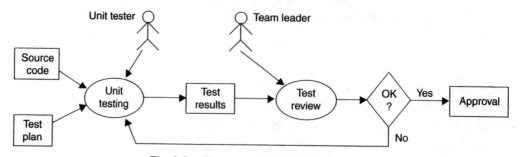

Fig. 2-2. Process model with decisions.

2.2 Data Flow Diagrams

One of the most basic diagrams in software development is the ***data flow diagram***. A data flow diagram shows the flow of the data among a set of components. The components may be tasks, software components, or even abstractions of the functionality that will be included in the software system. The actors are not included in the data flow diagram. The sequence of actions can often be inferred from the sequence of activity boxes.

The following are rules and interpretations for correct data flow diagrams:

1. Boxes are processes and must be verb phrases.

2. Arcs represent data and must be labeled with noun phrases.

3. Control is not shown. Some sequencing may be inferred from the ordering.

4. A process may be a one-time activity, or it may imply a continuous processing.

5. Two arcs coming out a box may indicate that both outputs are produced or that one or the other is produced.

EXAMPLE 2.3
The unit testing example from the previous section can be depicted as a data flow diagram, as shown in Fig. 2-3.

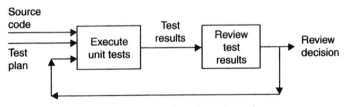

Fig. 2-3. Data flow for unit testing.

Figure 2-3 illustrates some of the rules. The phrases within the boxes are verb phrases. They represent actions. Each arrow/line is labeled with a noun phrase that represents some artifact.

The data flow diagram does not show decisions explicitly. The example shows that the results of testing can influence further testing and that the results of the test review action can also affect the testing (or retesting).

EXAMPLE 2.4
The calculation of the mathematical formula $(x + y) * (w + z)$ can be shown as a sequence of operations, as shown in Fig. 2-4:

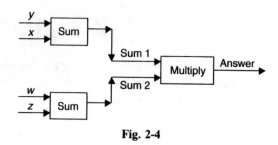

Fig. 2-4

2.3 Petri Net Models

The basic *petri net* model consists of condition nodes, arcs, event nodes, and tokens. If the input condition nodes for an event node all have tokens, then the event can fire, the tokens are removed from the input nodes, and tokens are placed on all of the output nodes of the firing position. The condition nodes are usually represented by circles and the event nodes by horizontal lines or rectangles.

In a petri net model, the condition nodes usually represent some required condition—for instance, the existence of a test plan. A token at the condition means that the condition is met. An event node (the horizontal line) represents an event that can happen (fire) when all the requirements are met (tokens in all the condition nodes). Tokens are then placed at all the condition nodes that follow the event.

EXAMPLE 2.5
A petri net model of testing is shown in Fig. 2-5.

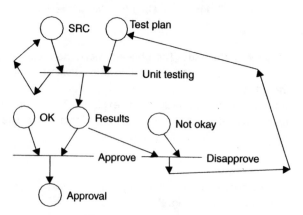

Fig. 2-5. Petri net model.

There are a number of different variations on the basic petri net model.

2.4   Object Models

In object-oriented development (Chapter 11), both the problem in the problem domain and the solution in the machine space are described in terms of objects. In the solution, these objects normally become classes. As the requirements and design phases of software development progress, the objects switch from being representations of the things in the problem domain to being programming structures in the software.

Object models represent entities and relationships between entities. Each box represents a type of object, and the name, attributes, and the methods of the object are listed inside the box. The top section of the box is for the name of the object, the second section is for the attributes, and the bottom section is for the methods. An arc between two objects represents a relationship between the objects. Arcs may be labeled in the center with a name of the association. The roles may be labeled at the opposite end. Also, at each end a multiplicity may be given indicating how many different associations of the same kind are allowed.

The three major types of relationships are (1) inheritance, (2) aggregation, and (3) association. An *inheritance* relationship implies that the object at the bottom of the arc is a special case of the object at the top of the arc. For example, the top object might be a vehicle and the bottom object a car, which is a kind of vehicle. This is often called an "is-a" relationship. An *aggregation* relationship implies that the object at the bottom of the arc is a component of the object at the top of the arc. For example, the top object might be a car and the bottom object might be the engine. This is often called a "part-of" relationship. The final type of relationship is an *association*, and this arc implies that somehow one of the objects is associated with the other object. For example, a "father-son" relationship is an association. This relationship may be two-way, or it might only be one-way.

Although there are many different notations, we will use a notation compatible with the Unified Modeling Language (UML) standard.[1]

EXAMPLE 2.6
Construct an object model for a library. The objects in the simple library shown in Fig. 2.6 consist of the library, books, copies of books, and patrons.

None of the methods of the objects are shown. The library has an aggregation relationship with **book** and with **patron**. That is, the library is really made up of books and patrons. The relationship between **book** and **copy** is neither aggregation nor inheritance. The object **book** represents the abstraction of a book, while the **copy** is the physical item that is loaned out. The relationship between patron and copy is called "loan." From the view of copy, the role is "checked out by" and from patron the role is "check out." The multiplicities indicate that a copy can either not be checked out or can have this relationship with only one patron at a time ("0.1"). The other multiplicity, "0.*", indicates that a patron can have zero or one or many relationships of "check out" at a time.

---

[1] See www.omg.org or www.rational.com or search for UML with your browser.

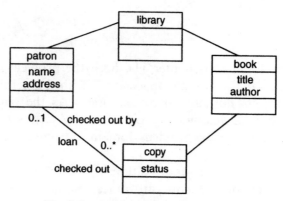

Fig. 2-6.   **Object model of simple library.**

EXAMPLE 2.7

Construct an object model for a family-tree system that stores genealogical information about family members.

Figure 2-7 indicates that everyone has a birthfamily. Every marriage has a father person and a mother person. Many attributes have been left off the diagram, and no functions are shown.

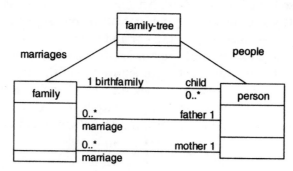

Fig. 2-7.   **Family-tree object model**

2.4.1   EXISTENCE DEPENDENCY[2]

One approach to clarifying the relationships is to introduce a different relationship called *existence dependency* (ED). Existence dependency relationships are defined as follows: A class (parent) can be associated with a lower class (child) if the lower (child) class only exists when the upper (parent) class exists and each instance of the lower (child) class is associated with exactly one instance of the upper (parent) class. This relationship and inheritance can be used to represent any problem domain.

---

[2] Snoeck and Dedene. "Existence Dependency: The Key to Semantic Integrity between Structural and Behavioral Aspects of Object Types." *IEEE TOSE*, April 1998.

EXAMPLE 2.8
Construct an object model for a library using the existence dependency relationships.

   As shown in Fig. 2-6 in example 2.6, all the relationships except "loan" and library-book satisfy the requirements of existence dependency. The relationship "loan" does not satisfy it, since a copy object can exist before the existence of the patron object that is checking it out. However, a loan object can be created that does satisfy the ED relationship. The object "book" cannot be a child of library, since books can exist before and after a specific library. "Person" is added to the diagram (see Fig. 2-8) to show the part of the patron that is not existence-dependent on "library."

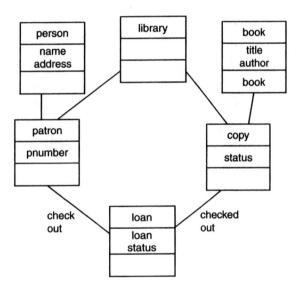

Fig. 2-8.   Library object model using ED.

2.4.2   INSTANCE DIAGRAMS

Object diagrams represent types of objects. Thus, a box labeled "car" represents the attributes and functions of all cars. Sometimes the relationships between instances of objects are not very clear in an object diagram. An *instance diagram* shows example instances of objects and may clarify the relationships.

EXAMPLE 2.9
Draw an instance model showing Fred, his wife Sue, their children Bill, Tom, and Mary, and his parents Mike and Jean. (See Fig. 2-9.)

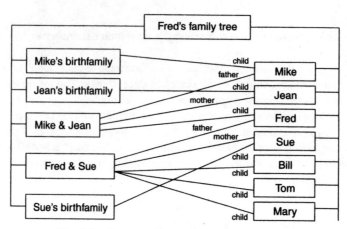

Fig. 2-9. Instance diagram of Fred's family tree.

2.5 Use Case Diagrams

A *use case* diagram is part of the UML set of diagrams. It shows the important actors and functionality of a system. Actors are represented by stick figures and functions by ovals. Actors are associated with functions they can perform.

EXAMPLE 2.10
Draw a use case diagram for the simple library. (See Fig. 2-10.)

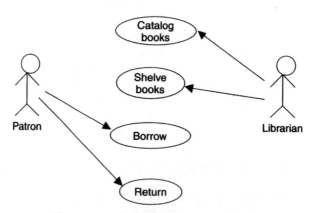

Fig. 2-10. Use case for simple library.

The functions in the ovals are methods of the classes in the object model. The patron object can borrow and return copies. The librarian actor is not an object on the object model. The librarian in the use case shows that some functions—for instance, catalog and shelve books—are not functions available to the patron.

2.6   Scenarios

A *scenario* is a description of one sequence of actions that could occur in this problem domain.

EXAMPLE 2.11
Write a scenario for the library problem.
   Fred, a patron, goes to the library and checks out a book. Two months later, he brings the overdue library book back to the library.

2.7   Sequence Diagrams

A *sequence diagram* is part of the UML set of diagrams. The diagram has vertical lines, which represent instances of classes. Each vertical line is labeled at the top with the class name followed by a colon followed by the instance name. For example, the first line is labeled with `lib:main` for the instance `main` of the class `library`. Horizontal arrows depict function calls. The tail of the arrow is on the line of the calling class, and the head of the arrow is on the line of the called class. The name of the function is on the arrow. The wide block on the vertical line shows the execution time of the called function. Returns are normally not shown. Multiple calls to the same function are often shown as just one arrow.

EXAMPLE 2.12
Draw a sequence diagram for the scenario of Example 2.11. (See Fig. 2-11.)

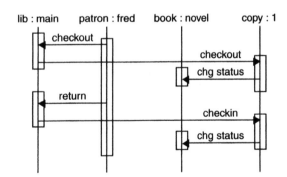

Fig. 2-11.   Sequence diagram for checkout scenario.

This diagram is much closer to the design phase than the object model presented in Example 2.8. There are functions used in this diagram that are not represented in the earlier object model. Also, the sequence of calls represented in this diagram is dependent on the actual design.

2.8   Hierarchy Diagrams

A **_hierarchy diagram_** shows the calling structure of a system. Each box represents a function. A line is drawn from one function to another function if the first function can call the second function. All possible calls are shown.

It is not one of the UML set of diagrams and is often not used in object-oriented development. However, it can be a very useful diagram to understand the dynamic structure of a system.

EXAMPLE 2.13
Draw a hierarchy diagram for the library program used in Example 2.12. (See Fig. 2-12.)

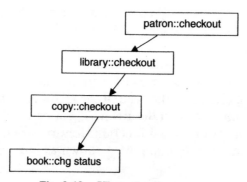

Fig. 2-12.   Hierarchy diagram.

2.9   Control Flow Graphs

A **_control flow graph_** (CFG) shows the control structure of code. Each node (circle) represents a block of code that has only one way through the code. That is, there is one entrance at the beginning of the block and one exit at the end. If any statement in the block is executed, then all statements in the block are executed. Arcs between nodes represent possible flows of control. That is, if it is possible that block B is executed, right after block A, then there must be an arc from block A to block B.

The following are rules for correct control flow diagrams:

1.   There must be one start node.
2.   From the start node, there must be a path to each node.
3.   From each node, there must be a path to a halt node.

EXAMPLE 2.14
Draw a control flow graph for the following triangle problem.

```
read x,y,z;
type = ''scalene'';
if (x == y or x == z or y == z) type =''isosceles'';
if (x == y and x == z) type =''equilateral'';
if (x >= y+z or y >= x+z or z >= x+y) type =''not a triangle'';
if (x <= 0 or y <= 0 or| z <= 0) type =''bad inputs'';
print type;
```

In Fig. 2-13, the ''a'' node represents the first two statements and the `if`
statement. The ''type = isosceles'' is in the node labeled ''isosceles''.
Similarly, the ''c'' node represents the next `if` statement, and the
''equilateral'' node represents the body of the `if`.

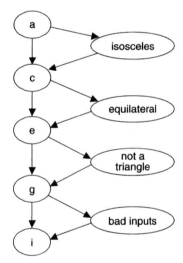

Fig. 2-13. Control flow graph for triangle program.

2.10   State Diagrams

The state of a machine or program is the collection of all the values of all the
variables, registers, and so on. A *state diagram* shows the states of the system and
the possible transitions between these states. A program or machine will have an
extremely large number of different states. However, many states will be similar in
how the machine will behave on the next input, and so forth. A group of states
with similar behaviors can be grouped together into a state. These states can be
diagrammed to show the transitions between the states. Many programs are best
described with a state diagram.

The following are rules for correct state diagrams:

1. There is one initial state.
2. Every state can be reached from the initial state.
3. From each state, there must be a path to a stop state.
4. Every transition between states must be labeled with an event that will cause that transition.

EXAMPLE 2.15
Draw a state diagram for a fixed-size stack. (See Fig. 2-14.)

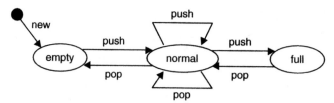

Fig. 2-14.   **State diagram for a fixed-size stack.**

There are two approaches to state diagrams. In Fig. 2-14, only legal or non-error transitions are specified. It is assumed that any transition that is not shown is illegal. For example, there is no push transition from the full state. Another approach is to show all transitions, including transitions that cause errors.

EXAMPLE 2.16
Draw a state diagram for a stack with all the error transitions shown. (See Fig. 2-15.)

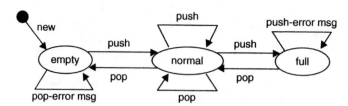

Fig. 2-15.   **State diagrams showing error transitions.**

State diagrams can be drawn directly from source code. Each function must be examined for decisions that are based on the values of variables (the state of the system).

EXAMPLE 2.17
The following code is for a push method on a finite stack:

```
int push(int item) {
    if (stackindex == MAX) {return ERROR;}
    stack[stackindex++] = item;
    return 0;
    }
```

From this code, two states with different behavior of the function can be identified. Note that the stackindex starts at zero. One state is related to the condition stackindex == MAX, and the other state is related to the condition stackindex != MAX. Analysis of the increment will show that the second state is stackindex < MAX (at least from this method). Analyzing the pop method will reveal the empty state of the stack.

2.11   Lattice Models

A *lattice* is a mathematical structure that shows set relationships. Although not used in software development very often, it is being used more to show the relationships between sets of functions and attributes.

EXAMPLE 2.18
Draw a lattice model for a stack implementation that has attributes for an array (s-array) and the index of the top element of the stack (index) and methods to push, pop, val (displays top value), and depth. (See Fig. 2-16.)

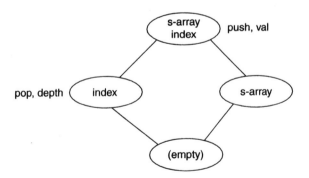

Fig. 2-16.   Lattice model for stack example.

The top node represents the set of all the attributes and the bottom node the empty set. The nodes are annotated with the names of the functions that use that subset of the attributes.

Review Questions

1. What are the differences between a software life cycle model and a process model?

2. What is the difference between a descriptive process model and a prescriptive process model?

3. Why are decisions more common in prescriptive process models than in descriptive process models?

4. Why should tasks in a process model be separated by an artifact?

5. Why can't a task in a process model start until its input artifacts exist?

6. Why does every node in a process model have to have a path from the start node to itself and a path from itself to a terminal node?

7. In Example 2.3, how can a person distinguish between a test review that only occurs after all the unit testing was complete and a test review that occurs after each module has been unit tested?

8. What do data flow diagrams specify about control flow?

9. When does a petri net firing position fire?

10. What happens when a petri net firing position fires?

11. What is the difference between the problem domain and the solution space?

12. What changes in an object model from requirements to design?

13. Classify each of the following relationships as either an inheritance relationship, an aggregation relationship, or a general association:

   Car—Lincoln Town car
   Person—Student
   Library—Library patron
   Book—Copy
   Car—Driver
   Patron—Book loan
   Class—Students

14. Classify each of the following as a class or an instance of a class:
   My automobile
   Person
   Fred
   Vehicle
   Professor
   The CIS department

15. What is the relationship between a scenario and a state diagram showing all possible sequences of actions?

16. In an interaction diagram, is the calling class or the called class at the head of the arrow?

17. Explain why the aggregation relation is a relation in the problem domain and not in the implementation domain.

18. Why don't data flow diagrams have rules about reachability between the nodes?

Problems

1. Draw a process model for the task of painting the walls in a room. Include the following tasks: choose color, buy paint, clean the walls, stir the paint, paint the wall.

2. The author uses interactive sessions when he teaches a course that includes distance learning students. The author divides the students into teams and posts a problem on the Web page. The teams work on the problem using chat rooms, ask questions of the instructor using a message board, and submit the solution via email. The instructor then grades the solutions using a grading sheet. Draw a process model for the interactive sessions.

3. Draw a data flow diagram for the simple library problem.

4. Draw a data flow diagram for a factory problem.

5. Draw a data flow diagram for a grocery store problem.

6. Draw an object model for a binary tree.

7. Draw an instance diagram of the binary tree object model.

8. Draw an object model for the grocery store problem.

9. Draw an object model for the factory problem.

10. Write additional scenarios for the patron checking out books from Example 2.11.

11. Draw a state diagram for a graphical user interface that has a main menu, a file menu with a file open command, and quit commands at each menu. Assume that only one file can be open at a time.

12. Extend the object model shown in Fig. 2-17 for the library problem to include a reservation object so patrons can reserve a book that has all copies checked out.

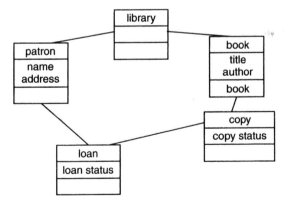

Fig. 2-17. Library problem object model.

13. Build a state machine for the library problem with the ability to reserve books.

Answers to Review Questions

1. What are the differences between a software life cycle model and a process model?

A software life cycle (SLC) model shows the major phases and the major deliverables, while a process model depicts the low-level tasks, the artifacts needed and produced, and the actors responsible for each low-level task.

2. What is the difference between a descriptive process model and a prescriptive process model?

A descriptive process model describes what has happened in a software development. It is often developed as the result of a postmortem analysis. A prescriptive model describes what should be done during software development, including responses to error situations.

3. Why are decisions more common in prescriptive process models than in descriptive process models?

Decisions are more common in prescriptive process models because a prescriptive process model is trying to cover what is done in alternative situations. Thus, it may need to specify the decision that is used to decide what to do next. A descriptive process model describes what happened, and alternative actions are usually not included.

4. Why should tasks in a process model be separated by an artifact?

If one process follows another process, some information or document from the first process is needed by the second. If this were not true, then the two processes would be independent of each other and one would not follow the other. This information or document should be identified and documented.

5. Why can't a task in a process model start until its input artifacts exist?

If one process depends on information from another, this second process cannot start until the first process is finished. Some other process notations allow concurrency between two tasks, where the first process has to start before the second process starts and the second process has to finish after the first process finishes.

6. Why does every node in a process model have to have a path from the start node to itself and a path from itself to a terminal node?

If there is not a path from a start node to every node, then some nodes in the process model are never reachable and can be eliminated. If there is not a path from the current node to the terminal node, then there is an infinite loop. Neither of these situations is desirable and they need to be investigated.

7. In Example 2.3, how can a person distinguish between a test review that only occurs after all the unit testing was complete and a test review that occurs after each module has been unit tested?

The label on the test results arrow implies that the output from the unit testing module has the results of more than one execution. Thus, it implies that the test review occurs only after multiple units are tested.

8. What do data flow diagrams specify about control flow?

Data flow diagrams do not specify control flow. Some sequence information may be inferred but nothing else.

9. When does a petri net firing position fire?

A petri net firing position fires when there is a token on every input node of the firing position.

10. What happens when a petri net firing position fires?

A token is placed on every output node of the firing position.

11. What is the difference between the problem domain and the solution space?

The problem domain is part of the real world and consists of entities that exist in the real world. The solution space consists of software entities in the implementation of the solution.

12. What changes in an object model from requirements to design?

Initially, the objects are entities in the problem domain. As the development moves into the design phase, those objects become entities in the solution space.

13. Classify each of the following relationships as either an inheritance relationship, an aggregation relationship, or a general association:

Car—Lincoln town car	Inheritance
Person—Student	Inheritance
Library—Library patron	Aggregation
Book—Copy	General association
Car—Driver	General association
Patron—Book loan	General association
Class—Students	Aggregation

14. Classify each of the following as a class or an instance of a class:

My automobile	Instance
Person	Class
Fred	Instance
Vehicle	Class
Professor	Class
The CIS department	Instance

15. What is the relationship between a scenario and a state diagram showing all possible sequences of actions?

The scenario would be just one path through part or all of the state diagram.

16. In an interaction diagram, is the calling class or the called class at the head of the arrow?

The called class is at the head of the arrow. The function on the arrow must be a function of the class at the head of arrow.

17. Explain why the aggregation relation is a relation in the problem domain and not in the implementation domain.

There is no difference in the implementation of an aggregation relation and other association relations. In fact, it can be hard to decide if some relations are really aggregations or not. For example, it is obvious that a car is an aggregation of the car's parts. However, it is not obvious whether a store should be considered an aggregation of customers.

18. Why don't data flow diagrams have rules about reachability between the nodes?

Data flow diagrams do not show control. Thus, two processes may not be linked in a data flow diagram. If each process uses different input data and produces different output data, and no output from one is used as an input for the other, there will not be an arc between them.

Answers to Problems

1. Draw a process model for the task of painting the walls in a room. Include the following tasks: choose color, buy paint, clean the walls, stir the paint, and paint the wall.

See Fig. 2-18.

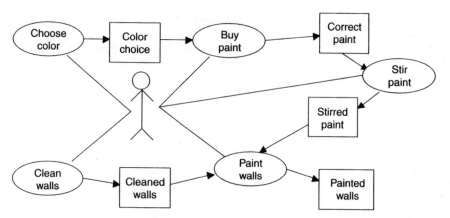

Fig. 2-18. Process model from painting walls.

2. The author uses interactive sessions when he teaches a course that includes distance learning students. The author divides the students into teams and posts a problem on the Web page. The teams work on the problem using chat rooms, ask questions of the instructor using a message board, and submit the solution via email. The instructor then grades the solutions using a grading sheet. Draw a process model for the interactive sessions.

See Fig. 2-19.

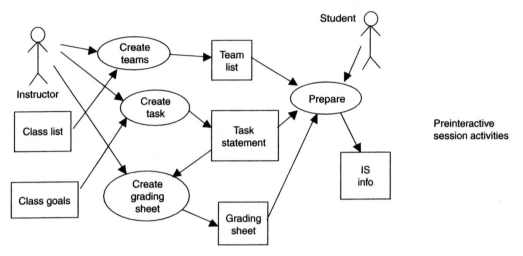

Process model for preparing for interactive session.

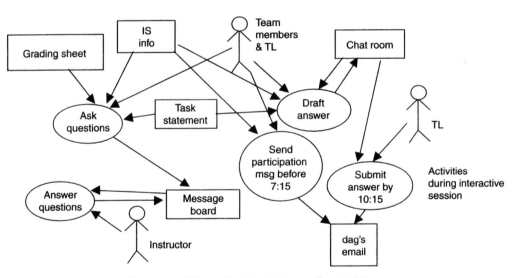

Process model for tasks during the interactive session.

Fig. 2-19

3. Draw a data flow diagram for the simple library problem.

See Fig. 2-20.

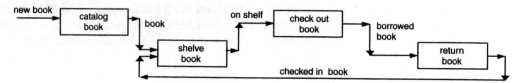

Fig. 2-20.   Data flow diagram for library problem.

4. Draw a data flow diagram for a factory problem.

See Fig. 2-21.

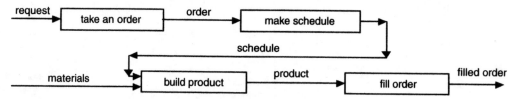

Fig. 2-21.   Factory problem data flow diagram.

5. Draw a data flow diagram for a grocery store.

See Fig. 2-22.

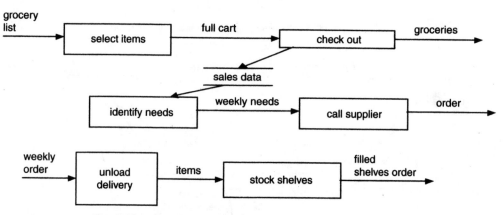

Fig. 2-22.   Grocery store data flow diagram.

6. Draw an object model for a binary tree.

See Fig. 2-23.

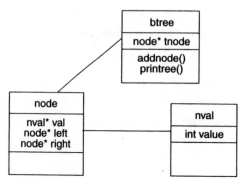

Fig. 2-23   Binary tree object model.

7. Draw an instance diagram of the binary tree object model.

See Fig. 2-24.

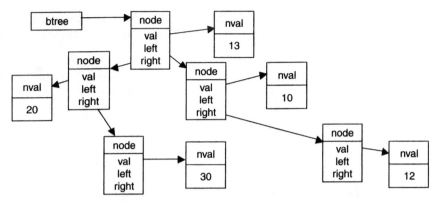

Fig. 2-24.   Instance diagram for binary tree.

8. Draw an object model for the grocery store problem.

See Fig. 2-25.

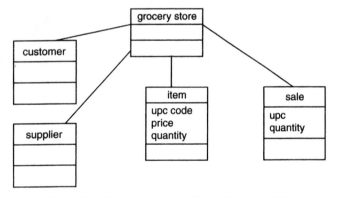

Fig. 2-25.   Grocery store problem object model.

9. Draw an object model for the factory problem.

See Fig. 2-26.

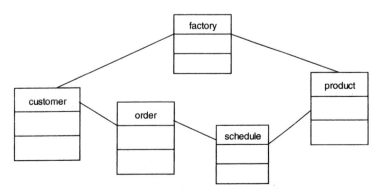

Fig. 2-26.   Factory object model.

10. Write additional scenarios for the patron checking out books from Example 2.11.

    Fred goes to the library and cannot find a book to check out.

    Fred goes to the library and checks out two books. Then he goes back to the library and checks out three more books. Fred returns the second three books on time. Fred returns the first two books late.

11. Draw a state diagram for a graphical user interface that has a main menu, a file menu with a file open command, and quit commands at each menu. Assume that only one file can be open at a time.

    See Fig. 2-27.

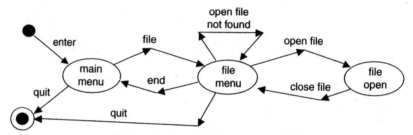

Fig. 2-27.   State diagram for GUI.

Note that "close file" was not mentioned in the problem spec but a transition out of the "file open" state is required.

12. Extend the following object model for the library problem to include a reservation object so patrons can reserve a book that has all copies checked out.

    See Fig. 2-28.

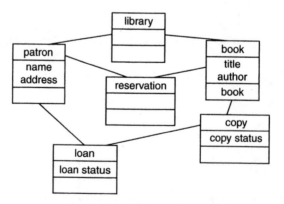

Fig. 2-28.   Library object model.

13. Build a state machine for the library problem with the ability to reserve books.

    See Fig. 2-29.

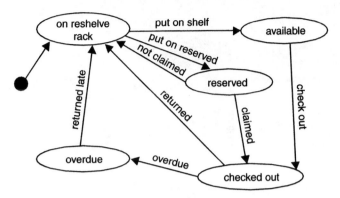

Fig. 2-29. State machine for library problem.

Software Project Management

3.1 Introduction

Although the word "manager" may remind many of us of the manager in the "Dilbert" comic strip, management is important. Software project management is the important task of planning, directing, motivating, and coordinating a group of professionals to accomplish software development. Software project management uses many concepts from management in general, but it also has some concerns unique to software development. One such concern is project visibility.

The lack of visibility of the software product during software development makes it hard to manage. In many other fields, it is easy to see progress or lack of progress. Many software projects get stalled at 90 percent complete. Ask any programmer if that bug that he or she found is the last bug in the software, and the answer will almost always be an emphatic yes. Many of the techniques in software management are aimed at overcoming this lack of visibility.

3.2 Management Approaches

A basic issue in software project management is whether the *process* or the *project* is the essential feature being managed. In process-oriented management, the management of the small tasks in the software life cycle is emphasized. In project management, the team achieving the project is emphasized. This results in important differences in viewpoint. In a *process* management approach, if the team does not follow the prescribed software life cycle, this would be a major difficulty. In a *project* management approach, success or failure is directly attributed to the team.

3.3 Team Approaches

Organizing a group of people into an efficient and effective team can be a difficult task. Letting a team develop its own paradigm can be risky. Choosing a team organization based on the project and the team members may help avoid disaster.

One aspect of a team is the amount of structure in the team. While some groups of programmers can work very independently, other groups need strong structure to make progress. The chief programmer team mentioned in the next section is an example of a strongly structured team. In a strongly structured team, small assignments are made to each member. These are often called "inch pebbles" because the assignments are small milestones. In a weakly structured team, the tasks are usually of longer duration and more open-ended.

Some teams consist of people with similar skills. These teams often stay together through many projects. Other teams are composed of people with different expertise that are grouped into a team based on the need for specific skills for a project. This is often called a **matrix organization**.

3.3.1 CHIEF PROGRAMMER TEAMS

IBM developed the chief programmer team concept. It assigns specific roles to members of the team. The chief programmer is the best programmer and leads the team. Nonprogrammers are used on the team for documentation and clerical duties. Junior programmers are included to be mentored by the chief programmer.

EXAMPLE 3.1
Draw a high-level process model for a hierarchical team organization. (See Fig. 3-1.)

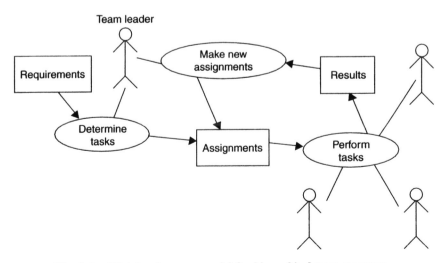

Fig. 3-1.   High-level process model for hierarchical team structure.

EXAMPLE 3.2

Company WRT has an IT department with a few experienced software developers and many new programmers. The IT manager has decided to use highly structured teams using a process approach to managing. Each team will be led by an experienced software developer. Each team member will be given a set of tasks weekly. The team leader will continually review progress and make new assignments.

3.4 Critical Practices

Most studies of software development have identified sets of practices that seem critical for success. The following 16 critical success practices come from the Software Project Managers Network (www.spmn.com):

- Adopt continuous risk management.
- Estimate cost and schedule empirically.
- Use metrics to manage.
- Track earned value.
- Track defects against quality targets.
- Treat people as the most important resource.
- Adopt life cycle configuration management.[1]
- Manage and trace requirements.
- Use system-based software design.
- Ensure data and database interoperability.
- Define and control interfaces.
- Design twice, code once.
- Assess reuse risks and costs.
- Inspect requirements and design.
- Manage testing as a continuous process.
- Compile and smoke-test frequently.

EXAMPLE 3.3

The IT manager of company WRT needs a software process that will aid his inexperienced software developers in successful software development. The manager uses the best-practices list to ensure that his software process will include important activities.

Practice 1: Adopt continuous risk management. The manager includes process steps throughout the life cycle in which the possible risks are identified and evaluated, and tasks are included to ameliorate the risks.

---

[1] A configuration management tool will store and safeguard multiple versions of source code and documentation. The user can retrieve any version.

Practice 2: *Estimate cost and schedule empirically.* The manager includes a process step to estimate the costs at the beginning of the life cycle and steps to reestimate the costs throughout the life cycle. Steps include archiving the data to be used for future estimation.

Practice 3: *Use metrics to manage.* The manager chooses metrics and includes steps for metric recording and steps for evaluating progress based on the metrics.

Practice 4: *Track earned value.* The manager includes steps to calculate earned value (see below) and to post the calculations.

Practice 5: *Track defects against quality targets.* The manager establishes goals for the number of defect reports that are received. Process steps for posting the number of defect reports are included.

Practice 6: *Treat people as the most important resource.* The manager reviews the whole software process to consider the impact on the programmer.

Practice 7: *Adopt life cycle configuration management.* The manager includes in the process the use of a configuration management tool for all documents and includes process steps to enter all documents and changes into the configuration management tool.

Practice 8: *Manage and trace requirements.* The manager includes process steps to acquire the requirements from the user and steps to trace each requirement to the current phase of development.

Practice 9: *Use system-based software design.* The manager includes steps to ensure a system-based design.

Practice 10: *Ensure data and database interoperability.* The manager includes steps to check for interoperability between the data and the database.

Practice 11: *Define and control interfaces.* The manager includes steps to define and baseline the interfaces.

Practice 12: *Design twice, code once.* The manager includes design review steps.

Practice 13: *Assess reuse risks and costs.* The manager includes steps to identify areas of potential reuse and steps to assess costs and risks.

Practice 14: *Inspect requirements and design.* The manager includes inspection steps in both the requirements and design phases.

Practice 15: *Manage testing as a continuous process.* The manager includes testing steps in all phases.

Practice 16: *Compile and smoke-test frequently.* The manager includes frequent testing steps in the implementation phase.

3.5   Capability Maturity Model

The Software Engineering Institute (*www.sei.cmu.edu*) has developed the Capability Maturity Models. The Software Engineering Capability Maturity Model (SE-CMM) is used to rate an organization's software development process. An assessment of an organization's practices, processes, and organization is used to classify an organization at one of the following levels:

- **Level 1: Initial**—This is the lowest level and usually characterized as chaotic.

- **Level 2: Repeatable**—This level of development capability includes project tracking of costs, schedule, and functionality. The capability exists to repeat earlier successes.

- **Level 3: Defined**—This level has a defined software process that is documented and standardized. All development is accomplished using the standard processes.

- **Level 4: Managed**—This level quantitatively manages both the process and the products.

- **Level 5: Optimizing**—This level uses the quantitative information to continuously improve and manage the software process.

Most organizations will be assessed at level 1 initially. Improving to higher levels involves large efforts at organization and process management. Level 5 has been achieved by only a few organizations.

3.6 Personal Software Process

Watts Humphrey[2] has developed the Personal Software Process to improve the skills of the individual software engineer. His approach has the individual maintain personal time logs to monitor and measure the individual's skills. One result of this is measuring an individual's productivity. The usual measure of productivity is lines of code produced per day (LOC/day). Additionally, errors are timed and recorded. This allows an individual to learn where errors are made and to assess different techniques for their effect on productivity and error rates. Additionally, the productivity can be used to evaluate the reasonableness of proposed schedules.

EXAMPLE 3.4
Programmer X recorded this time log.

Date	Start	Stop	Interruptions	Delta	Task
1/1/01	09:00	15:30	30 lunch	360	Code 50 LOC
1/3/01	09:00	14:00	30 lunch	270	Code 60 LOC
1/4/01	09:00	11:30		150	Code 50 LOC
	12:00	14:00		120	testing

---

[2] W. Humphrey. *Introduction to the Personal Software Process.* Addison-Wesley, 1997.

The programmer spent 360 + 270 + 150 + 120 = 900 minutes to write and test a program of 160 LOC. Assuming 5 hours per day (300 minutes/day), X spent effectively 3 days to program 160 LOC. This gives a productivity of 53 LOC/day. When X's manager schedules a week to code a 1000 = LOC project, X is able to estimate that the project will take about 4 weeks.

3.7   Earned Value Analysis

One approach to measuring progress in a software project is to calculate how much has been accomplished. This is called *earned value analysis*. It is basically the percentage of the estimated time that has been completed. Additional measures can be calculated.

Although this is based on estimated effort, it could be based on any quantity that can be estimated and is related to progress.

3.7.1   BASIC MEASURES

- *Budgeted Cost of Work (BCW)*: The estimated effort for each work task.
- *Budgeted Cost of Work Scheduled (BCWS)*: The sum of the estimated effort for each work task that was scheduled to be completed by the specified time.
- *Budget at Completion (BAC)*: The total of the BCWS and thus the estimate of the total effort for the project.
- *Planned Value (PV)*: The percentage of the total estimated effort that is assigned to a particular work task; PV = BCW/BAC.
- *Budgeted Cost of Work Performed (BCWP)*: The sum of the estimated efforts for the work tasks that have been completed by the specified time.
- *Actual Cost of Work Performed (ACWP)*: The sum of the actual efforts for the work tasks that have been completed.

3.7.2   PROGRESS INDICATORS

- Earned Value (EV) = BCWP/BAC
            = The sum of the PVs for all completed work tasks
            = PC = Percent complete
- Schedule Performance Index (SPI) = BCWP/BCWS
- Schedule Variance (SV) = BCWP − BCWS
- Cost Performance Index (CPI) = BCWP/ACWP
- Cost Variance (CV) = BCWP − ACWP

EXAMPLE 3.5
Company LMN is partway through its project. The job log below indicates the current status of the project.

Work Task	Estimated Effort (programmer-days)	Actual Effort So Far (programmer-days)	Estimated Completion Date	Actual Date Completed
1	5	10	1/25/01	2/1/01
2	25	20	2/15/01	2/15/01
3	120	80	5/15/01	
4	40	50	4/15/01	4/1/01
5	60	50	7/1/01	
6	80	70	9/01/01	

The BAC is the sum of the estimations. BAC = 330 days. BAC is an estimate of the total work. On 4/1/01, tasks 1,2, and 4 have been completed. The BCWP is the sum of the BCWS for those tasks. So BCWP is 70 days. The earned value (EV) is 70/330, or 21.2 percent. On 4/1/01 tasks 1 and 2 were scheduled to be completed and 1,2, and 4 were actually completed. So BCWP is 70 days and BCWS is 30 days. Thus, SPI is 70/30, or 233 percent. The SV = 70 days −30 days = +40 days, or 40 programmer-days ahead. The ACWP is the sum of actual effort for tasks 1, 2, and 4. So, ACWP is 80 programmer-days. CPI is 70/80 = 87.5 percent. The CV = 70 programmer-days −80 programmer-days = −10 programmer-days, or 10 programmer-days behind.

EXAMPLE 3.6
On 7/1/01, assume that task 3 has also been completed using 140 days of actual effort, so BCWP is 190 and EV is 190/330, or 57.5 percent. On 7/1/01, tasks 1, 2, 3, and 4 were actually completed. So BCWP is 190 days and BCWS is 250 days. Thus, SPI is 190/250 = 76 percent. The SV is 190 programmer-days −250 programmer-days = −60 programmer-days, or 60 programmer days behind. ACWP is the sum of actual effort for 1, 2, 3, and 4. So ACWP is 220 programmer-days. Tasks 1 through 5 were scheduled to have been completed, but only 1 through 4 were actually completed. CPI is 190/220 = 86.3 percent, and CV is 190−220, or 30 programmer-days behind.

3.8   Error Tracking

One excellent management practice is *error tracking*, which is keeping track of the errors that have occurred and the inter-error times (the time between occurrences of the errors). This can be used to make decisions about when to release software. An additional effect of tracking and publicizing the error rate is to make the software developers aware of the significance of errors and error reduction. The effects of changes in the software process can be seen in the error data. Additionally, making the errors and error detection visible encourages testers and developers to keep error reduction as a goal.

The error rate is the inverse of the inter-error time. That is, if errors occur every 2 days, then the instantaneous error rate is 0.5 errors/day. The current instantaneous error rate is a good estimate of the current error rate. If the faults that cause errors are not removed when the errors are found, then the cumulative error rate (the sum of all the errors found divided by the total time) is a good estimate of future error rates. Usually, most errors are corrected (the faults removed), and thus the error rates should go down and the inter-error times should be increasing. Plotting this data can show trends in the error rate (errors found per unit time). Fitting a straight line to the points is an effective way to display the trend. The trend can be used to estimate future error rates. When the trend crosses the x-axis, the estimate of the error rate is zero, or there are no more errors. If the x-axis is number of errors, the value of the x-intercept can be used as an estimate of the total number of errors in the software. If the x-axis is the elapsed time of testing, the intercept is an estimate of the testing time necessary to remove all errors. The area under this latter line is an estimate of the number of errors originally in the software.

EXAMPLE 3.7
Consider the following error data (given as the times between errors): 4, 3, 5, 6, 4, 6, 7. The instantaneous error rates are the inverses of the inter-error times: 0.25, 0.33, 0.20, 0.17, 0.25, 0.17, and 0.14. Plotting these against error number gives a downward curve, as shown in Figure 3-2. This suggests that the actual error rate is decreasing.

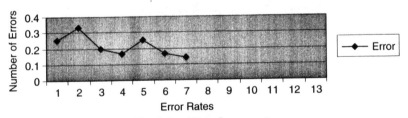

Fig. 3-2.   **Plot of error rates.**

A straight line through the points would intersect the axis about 11. Since this implies that the error rate would go to zero at the eleventh error, an estimate of the total number of errors in this software would be 11 errors. Since seven errors have been found, this suggests that there may be four more errors in the software.

3.9   Postmortem Reviews

One critical aspect of software development is to learn from your mistakes and successes. In software development, this is called a *postmortem*. It consists of

Project Name **Project X**	Start Date—Sept. 5, 00	Completion Date – Dec 8, 00
Management measures	Size | Estimated	Actual
---	---
3000 LOC	**5000 LOC**		Effort 	Estimated	Actual
---	---
12,000 min	**10,000 min**	
Subjective comments on estimation	Good **Effort was close in total.**	Bad **Imp effort was underestimated.**
Subjective comments on process	Good	Bad **Team members did not complete asgn on time.**
Subjective comments on schedule	Good	Bad **Not enough time for imp.**
Quality	Errors found. 	Req	Design	Unit	Integ	Postdel
---	---	---	---	---
			30						ave	max
mccabe	**4**	**30**
Method/class	**6**	**10**
Attributes/class	**10**	**15**
LOC/class	**150**	**500**	
Subjective comments on quality	Good	Bad **System not tested well.**
Problem: **Initial req ambiguity**	Description: **Format of input file was initially wrong**	Impact: **2 weeks wasted**
Problem:	Description:	Impact:
Problem:	Description:	Impact:
Problem:	Description:	Impact:

assembling key people from the development and the users groups. Issues consist of quality, schedule, and software process. It is important that everyone feel free to express opinions. A formal report needs to be produced and distributed. The reports should not be sanitized.

EXAMPLE 3.8
Company JKL produced the postmortem report shown on p. 38.

Review Questions

1. What is meant by visibility?
2. What is the difference between a process approach and a project approach?
3. For a new project that is very different from any previous project, would a process or project management approach be better?
4. What is the advantage of making many small, "inch-pebble" assignments?
5. Which earned value progress measures can decrease during a project?
6. For which of the earned value progress measures is a value greater than 1 good?
7. What would be the advantage of using the inverse of SPI and CPI?

Problems

1. Draw a process model for a team that has a weak structure and depends on the team discussions to set directions and resolve issues.
2. Using the following time log, calculate the programmer's productivity in LOC/day. Assume that project 1 was 120 LOC and project 2 was 80 LOC.

Date	Start	Stop	Interruptions	Delta	Task
2/1/01	08:30	16:30	60 lunch		Proj 1 coding
2/2/01	09:00	17:00	30 lunch		Proj 1 coding
2/5/01	09:00	17:30	30 lunch, 60 mtg		Proj 2 coding
2/6/01	07:30	12:00			Proj 2 coding

3. Using the following job log, calculate all of the basic measures and the progress indicators. Is the project on schedule? Assume that it is currently 5/01/01.

Work Task	Estimated Effort (programmer-days)	Actual Effort So Far (programmer-days)	Estimated Completion Date	Actual Date Completed
1	50	70	1/15/01	2/1/01
2	35	20	2/15/01	2/15/01
3	20	40	2/25/01	3/1/01
4	40	40	4/15/01	4/1/01
5	60	10	6/1/01	
6	80	20	7/1/01	

4. Use a spreadsheet to calculate the PV and the progress indicators for the following project at half-month intervals from January 1 through September 1.

Work Task	Estimated Effort (programmer-days)	Actual Effort (programmer-days)	Estimated Completion Date	Actual Date Completed
1	30	37	1/1	2/1
2	25	24	2/15	2/15
3	30	41	3/1	3/15
4	50	47	4/15	4/1
5	60	63	5/1	4/15
6	35	31	5/15	6/1
7	55	58	6/1	6/1
8	30	28	6/15	6/15
9	45	43	7/1	7/15
10	25	29	8/1	8/15
11	45	49	8/15	9/1

5. A professor has 40 homework assignments and 40 exams to grade. The exams usually take 3 times as long to grade as the homework assignments. Calculate the PV for each homework and for each exam. After 5 hours, if the professor has half of the exams done, how long should he estimate it will take to complete the grading?

6. Given the following inter-error times (that is, the time between occurrences of errors), use plots to estimate the total original number of errors and the time to completely remove all errors: 6, 4, 8, 5, 6, 9, 11, 14, 16, 19.

7. The project started on January 1 and should be finished by June 1. It is now March 1. Complete the following table. Calculate EV, SPI, SV, and CV. Determine whether the project is on time. Justify your answer. Show your work.

Job #	Est. Time	Actual Time Spent	PV	Due Date	Completed
1	30	10		Feb. 1	
2	20	30		Mar. 1	Yes
3	50	30		May 1	Yes
4	100	5		Jun. 1	

Answers to Review Questions

1. What is meant by visibility?

   Visibility is the attribute of being able to see the progress or lack of progress in a project.

2. What is the difference between a process approach and a project approach?

   A process approach is similar to an assembly line, where each person has a task to be done. Developers may do the same task on multiple projects—for example, a test team or a design team. A project emphasis would give the team the responsibility for the whole effort in developing a project.

3. For a new project that is very different from any previous project, would a process or project management approach be better?

   Process management works well with projects that are well understood. A new, very different project might be better managed by a project approach that emphasizes success in the project.

4. What is the advantage of making many small, "inch-pebble" assignments?

If a deadline or assignment is missed, the project is behind. The smaller the time between deadlines, the sooner it is evident if a project is behind. It is said that a project can only slip the length of an assignment before the manager can see the delay.

5. Which earned value progress measures can decrease during a project?

All but the earned value, which must increase.

6. For which of the earned value progress measures is a value greater than 1 good?

For SPI and SV, a value greater than 1 implies that more is being accomplished than was scheduled. For CPI and CV, a value greater than 1 implies that effort is less than what was estimated. So all four of these are good if their values are greater than 1.

7. What would be the advantage of using the inverse of SPI and CPI?

The inverse of each could be used as a projection tool. If the inverse of SPI was 2, it would imply that project will take twice as long as estimated. If the inverse of CPI was 2, it would imply that the project will take twice the effort that was estimated.

Answers to Problems

1. Draw a process model for a team that has a weak structure and depends on the team discussions to set directions and resolve issues.

See Fig. 3-3.

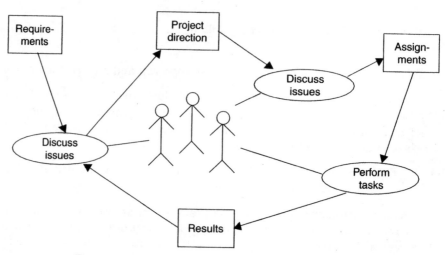

Fig. 3-3. Process model for team with weak structures.

2. Using the following time log, calculate the programmer's productivity in LOC/day. Assume that project 1 was 120 LOC and project 2 was 80 LOC.

Date	Start	Stop	Interruptions	Delta	Task
2/1/01	08:30	16:30	60 lunch		Proj 1 coding
2/2/01	09:00	17:00	30 lunch		Proj 1 coding
2/5/01	09:00	17:30	30 lunch, 60 mtg		Proj 2 coding
2/6/01	07:30	12:00			Proj 2 coding

The delta time for day 1 is 8 hours −1 hour for lunch = 420 minutes; day 2 is 8 hours −30 minutes = 450 minutes. So the productivity for project 1 is 120 LOC/ 870 minutes = 120 LOC/ 2.175 days = 55 LOC/programmer-day (assume 400 minutes per programmer day). The delta times for day 3 and 4 are 7 hours and 4.5 hours = 690 minutes. The productivity is 80 LOC/ 1.725 days = 46.4 LOC/programmer-day. Overall, the programmer averaged 200 LOC/ 3.9 days = 51.3 LOC/programmer-day.

3. Using the following job log, calculate all of the basic measures and the progress indicators. Is the project on schedule? Assume that it is currently 5/01/01.

Work Task	Estimated Effort (programmer-days)	Actual Effort So Far (programmer-days)	Estimated Completion Date	Actual Date Completed
1	50	70	1/15/01	2/1/01
2	35	20	2/15/01	2/15/01
3	20	40	2/25/01	3/1/01
4	40	40	4/15/01	4/1/01
5	60	10	6/1/01	
6	80	20	7/1/01	

The BCWS is $50+35+20+40=145$ programmer-days. The BAC is $50+35+20+40+60+80=285$ programmer-days. The planned values (PVs) for the work tasks are 17.5 percent, 12.3 percent, 7.0 percent, 14.0 percent, 21.1 percent, 28.1 percent. The earned value is 17.5 percent + 12.3 percent + 7 percent + 14 percent = 50.7 percent. The BCWP for 5/01/01 is the same as BCWS in this example because the scheduled work has been completed. Thus, SPI = 145/145 = 1.

The schedule variance is 145 −145＝0. The cost performance index ＝ 145 /170 ＝ 85.3 percent. This indicates that the actual effort is larger than the estimated effort. The cost variance is 145 −170＝−25. This also indicates that more effort has been required than was estimated.

The project appears to be on schedule but is costing more than was planned.

4. Use a spreadsheet to calculate the PV and the progress indicators for the following project at half-month intervals from January 1 through September 1.

Work Task	Estimated Effort (programmer-days)	Actual Effort (programmer-days)	Estimated Completion Date	Actual Date Completed
1	30	37	1/1	2/1
2	25	24	2/15	2/15
3	30	41	3/1	3/15
4	50	47	4/15	4/1
5	60	63	5/1	4/15
6	35	31	5/15	6/1
7	55	58	6/1	6/1
8	30	28	6/15	6/15
9	45	43	7/1	7/15
10	25	29	8/1	8/15
11	45	49	8/15	9/1

```
       bcw   pv    acw  sched   actual
 1  30  0.070  37   1-Jan  1-Feb
 2  25  0.058  24  15-Feb 15-Feb
 3  30  0.070  41   1-Mar 15-Mar
 4  50  0.116  47  15-Apr  1-Apr
 5  60  0.140  63   1-May 15-Apr
 6  35  0.081  31  15-May  1-Jun
 7  55  0.128  58   1-Jun  1-Jun
 8  30  0.070  28  15-Jun 15-Jun
 9  45  0.105  43   1-Jul 15-Jul
10  25  0.058  29   1-Aug 15-Aug
11  45  0.105  49  15-Aug  1-Sep
BAC 430
```

	bcws	bcwp	acwp	ev	spi	sv	cpi	cv
1-Jan	30	0	0	0.00		0	-30	0	0
15-Jan	30	0	0	0.00	0	-30	0	0
1-Feb	30	30	37	0.07	1.00	0	0.81	-7
15-Feb	55	55	61	0.13	1.00	0	0.90	-6
1-Mar	85	55	61	0.13	0.65	-30	0.90	-6
15-Mar	85	85	102	0.20	1.00	0	0.83	-17
1-Apr	85	135	149	0.31	1.59	50	0.91	-14
15-Apr	135	195	212	0.45	1.44	60	0.92	-17
1-May	195	195	212	0.45	1.00	0	0.92	-17
15-May	230	195	212	0.45	0.85	-35	0.92	-17
1-Jun	285	285	301	0.66	1.00	0	0.95	-16
15-Jun	315	315	329	0.73	1.00	0	0.96	-14
1-Jul	360	315	329	0.73	0.88	-45	0.96	-14
15-Jul	360	360	372	0.84	1.00	0	0.97	-12
1-Aug	385	360	372	0.84	0.94	-25	0.97	-12
15-Aug	430	385	401	0.90	0.90	-45	0.96	-16
1-Sep	430	430	450	1.00	1.00	0	0.96	-20

5. A professor has 40 homework assignments and 40 exams to grade. The exams usually take 3 times as long to grade as the homework assignments. Calculate the PV for each homework and for each exam. After 5 hours, if the professor has half of the exams done, how long should he estimate it will take to complete the grading?

Assume a grading unit is equal to 1 homework assignment. Then this task has a total of $40 * 1 + 40 * 3 = 160$ grading units. Each homework has a planned value of $1/160 = 0.625$ percent, and each exam has a planned value of 1.875 percent. After 5 hours, 20 exams are completed, or 37.5 percent. Thus, $5/0.375 = 13.33$ hours as the estimated total time, or 8.33 hours left.

6. Given the following inter-error times (that is, the time between occurrences of errors), use plots to estimate the total original number of errors and the time to completely remove all errors.

$$6, 4, 8, 5, 6, 9, 11, 14, 16, 19$$

The inverses of the inter-error times are the instantaneous error rates. Plotting these rates against the error number gives a plot that shows a trend of decreasing error rates, as shown in Fig. 3-4.

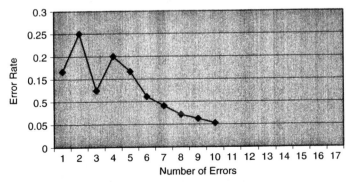

Fig. 3-4. Error rate plot.

Fitting a straight line would show an x-intercept of about 15. Using this as an estimate of the total number of original errors, we estimate that there are still five errors in the software.

The error rates can also be plotted against elapsed time (the sum of the previous inter-error times), as shown in Fig. 3-5.

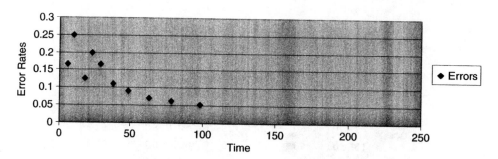

Fig. 3-5. Error rates vs. elapsed time.

Fitting a straight line to these points would give an x-intercept near 160. This would give an additional testing time of 62 units to remove all errors. The y-intercept would be around 0.25. The area under this line would be $0.5 * 160 * 0.25$, or 20 errors. This would suggest about 10 errors left. The differences between these two estimates show the roughness of this approach.

7. The project started on January 1 and should be finished by June 1. It is now March 1. Complete the following table. Calculate EV, SPI, SV, and CV. Determine whether the project is on time. Justify your answer. Show your work.

Job #	Est. Time	Actual Time Spent	PV	Due Date	Completed
1	30	10	.15	Feb. 1	
2	20	30	.10	Mar. 1	Yes
3	50	30	.25	May 1	Yes
4	100	5	.50	Jun. 1	

$BAC = 200$ $BCWS = 50$ $BCWP = 70$ $ACWP = 60$

$EV = 70/200 = 0.35$ $SV = 70 - 50 = 20$ $SPI = 70/50 = 1.4$ $CV = 70 - 60 = 10$

The project is ahead of schedule.

CHAPTER 4

Software Project Planning

4.1 Project Planning

Planning is essential and software development is no exception. Achieving success in software development requires planning. Software project planning involves deciding what tasks need to be done, in what order to do the tasks, and what resources are needed to accomplish the tasks.

4.2 WBS—Work Breakdown Structure

One of the first tasks is to break the large tasks into small tasks. It means finding identifiable parts of the tasks. It also means finding *deliverables* and *milestones* that can be used to measure progress.

The work breakdown structure (WBS) should be a tree structure. The top-level breakdown usually matches the life cycle model (LCM) used in the organization. The next-level breakdown can match the processes in the organization's process model (PM). Further levels are used to partition the task into smaller, more manageable tasks.

The following are rules for constructing a proper work breakdown structure:

1. *The WBS must be a tree structure.* There should be no loops or cycles in the WBS. Iterative actions will be shown in the process model and/or the life cycle model.

2. *Every task and deliverable description must be understandable and unambiguous.* The purpose of a WBS is communication with team members. If the team members misinterpret what the task or deliverable is supposed to be, there will be problems.

3. ***Every task must have a completion criterion (often a deliverable)***.   There must be a way to decide when a task is completed, because subtasks that have no definite ending encourage false expectations of progress. This decision is called a ***completion criterion***. It may be a deliverable, for example, a complete design for the project, and then a peer review can decide if it is complete.

4. ***All deliverables (artifacts) must be identified***.   A deliverable must be produced by some task or it won't be produced.

5. ***Positive completion of the tasks must imply completion of the whole task***.   The purpose of the work breakdown schedule is to identify the subtasks necessary to complete the whole task. If important tasks or deliverables are missing, the whole task will not be accomplished.

EXAMPLE 4.1
In making a loaf of bread, the life cycle model for cooking might be as shown in Fig. 4-1.

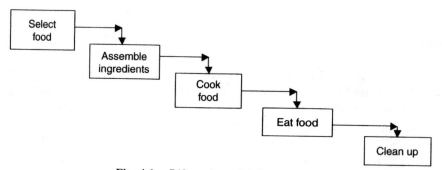

Fig. 4-1.   Life cycle model for cooking.

The process model for cooking might be as shown in Fig. 4-2.

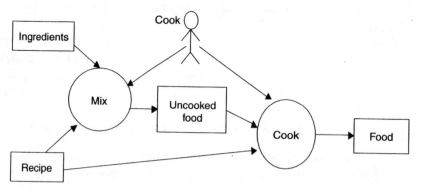

Fig. 4-2.   Cooking process model.

The subtasks might be as follows:
   Choose ingredients, Check on ingredients, Assemble ingredients, Add liquids, Add yeast, Add small amount of flour, Make sponge (yeast and liquids), Let rise

first time, Add remaining flour, Knead, Let rise second time, Form into loaves, Let rise third time, Bake, Slice, Butter, Eat, and Clean up.

These can be divided into the phases of the life cycle model and processes of the process model (the leftmost are LCMs, those with one indent are PMs, those with two indents are tasks, and the deliverables are on the right):

Select food
      Choose ingredients   List of ingredients
      Check on ingredients   Shopping list

Assemble ingredients
      Assemble ingredients   Assembled ingredients

Cook food
  Mix
      Add liquids   Liquid in bowl
      Add yeast   Liquids with yeast
      Add small amount of flour   Liquids and flour
      Make sponge (yeast and liquids)   Sponge
      Let rise first time   Risen sponge
      Add remaining flour and knead Kneaded dough
      Let rise second time   Risen dough
      Form into loaves   Loaves
      Let rise third time   Risen loaves

  Cook
      Bake   Bread

  Eat
      Slice   Slice of bread
      Butter   Buttered slice
      Eat   Good taste

  Clean up
      Clean up   Clean kitchen

EXAMPLE 4.2

Team XYZ wants to develop a face recognition system for use on the robot. The system is intended to greet visitors to the robotics laboratory. It should recognize faces it has seen before with a reasonable reliability. The first pass on the work breakdown might recognize the following subtasks:

Feasibility
    Determine feasibility of vision.
    Determine camera and software availability.
    Schedule camera and vision software acquisition.
Risk Analysis
    Determine vision risks.
Requirements
    Specify requirements.
Design
    Design prototypes.
    Prototype vision.

Implementation
Code the image capture.
Code the image processing.
Code the image comparison.
Integrate with other robot software.
Testing
Test image capture.
Delivery
Document.

Some of these subtasks are still very high level. These tasks may not have an obvious and checkable deliverable. That is, it may not be easy to determine definitively when a subtask has been completed. It is not suitable for a subtask to be done when the developer feels that it is done. There must be some way to determine objectively when a subtask has been completed properly.

EXAMPLE 4.3
The team broke the subtask "Code the image capture" into a more detailed set of subtasks, with each new subtask having a more specific deliverable and completion criterion. The set of subtasks and deliverables are the following:

Install commercial camera driver.	Installed driver
Test driver from windows and save an image to file.	Image file
Write routine to call driver from C++.	Routine
Test C++ routine separately and save an image to file.	Image from C++ code
Test C++ routine from the main robot control software and capture image.	Image from main

4.3 PERT—Program Evaluation and Review Technique

This technique creates a graph that shows the dependencies among the tasks. Each task has an estimate of the time necessary to complete the task and a list of other tasks that have to be completed before this task can be started (dependencies). The graph may not always have only one starting subtask or only one stopping subtask. The whole task is only completed when all the subtasks are completed. The graph can be used to calculate the *completion* times for all the subtasks, the minimum completion time for the whole task, and the *critical path* of the subtasks.

4.3.1 ALGORITHM FOR COMPLETION TIMES

1. For each node, do step 1.1 (until completion times of all nodes are calculated)
   1.1 If the predecessors are completed, then take the latest completions time of the predecessors and add required time for this node.

2. The node with the latest completion time determines the earliest completion time for project.

EXAMPLE 4.4

Apply this algorithm to Table 4-1, which shows an example of tasks and dependencies. The same dependencies are shown in Fig. 4-3. To apply the completion time algorithm, start with subtask a; it has no dependencies, so it can start at the initial time (say, 0). It can complete at time $0 + 8 = 8$. Similarly, subtask b can complete at time $0 + 10 = 10$. See Table 4-2. Note that since these subtasks are not dependent on each other or on anything else, they can start at time 0. Their completion times are calculated without concern for lack of resources. That is, for this completion calculation, it assumes that there are people available to do both tasks at the same time.

Table 4-1   Subtasks

Subtask ID	Time to Complete Task	Dependencies
a	8	
b	10	
c	8	a,b
d	9	a
e	5	b
f	3	c,d
g	2	d
h	4	f,g
i	3	e,f

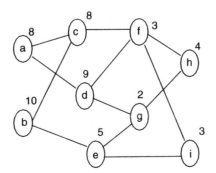

Fig. 4-3.   PERT diagram.

Table 4-2

Subtask ID	Start Time	Completion Time	Critical Path
a	0	8	
b	0	10	*
c	10	18	*
d	8	17	
e	10	15	
f	18	21	*
g	17	19	
h	21	25	*
i	21	24	

Since the completion times for subtasks a and b are now calculated, the completion times for nodes c, d, and e can be calculated. Since the predecessors of c finish at 8 and 10, subtask c can start at 10 and complete at 10 + 8 = 16. The start time for d will be 8 and the completion time can be 8 + 9 = 17, and for e the times will be 10 and 10 + 5 = 14.

Now we can process subtasks f and g. The start times can be 17 and 16, respectively. The completion times will be 17 + 3 = 20 for f and 16 + 2 = 18 for g. Subtasks h and i can now be calculated with both starting at 21 and h competing at 25 and i at 24. Table 4-2 has all of the start and completion times.

4.3.2 CRITICAL PATH

The *critical path* is the set of tasks that determines the shortest possible completion time. The completion time will be longer if there are insufficient resources to do all parallel activities. However, the completion time can never be made shorter by adding more resources.

4.3.3 ALGORITHM FOR MARKING CRITICAL PATH

1. Start with the node(s) with the latest completion time(s); mark it (them) as critical.

2. Select the predecessor(s) of the critical node(s) with latest completion time(s); mark it (them) as critical. Continue Step 2 until reaching the starting node(s).

EXAMPLE 4.5

In Table 4-2 we can see the completion times of all of the subtasks. Subtask h has the latest completion time, 25. Thus, we mark h as part of the critical path. The predecessors of h are f and g. Subtask f has the latest completion time of those two subtasks, so f is marked as part of the critical path.

Subtask f has c and d as predecessors. Since c has the later completion time, c is marked as part of the critical path. Subtask c has a and b as predecessors, and since b has the later time, it is part of the critical path. Since we are now at an initial subtask, the critical path is complete.

4.3.4   SLACK TIME

Subtasks that are on the critical path have to be started as early as possible or else the whole project will be delayed. However, subtasks that are not on the critical path have some flexibility on when they are started. This flexibility is called the *slack time*.

4.3.5   ALGORITHM FOR SLACK TIME

1. Pick the noncritical node with the latest ending time that has not been processed. If the subtask has no successors, pick the latest ending time of all nodes. If the subtask has successors, pick the earliest of the latest start times of the successor nodes. This is the latest completion time for this subtask. Make the latest start time for this subtask to reflect this time.
2. Repeat Step 1 until all noncritical path subtasks have been processed.

EXAMPLE 4.6

The noncritical subtask with the latest completion time is subtask i. Since it has no successors, the latest completion time, 25, is used. This is added as the latest completion time for i. Since 25 is 1 later than 24, the start time is changed from 21 to 21,22. Now the latest nonprocessed, noncritical subtask is g. Since h is the only successor of g, and h must start by 21, g must end by 21. So the completion time of g becomes 19,21 and the start time becomes 17,19. The next subtask to be processed will be d. It has successors f and g. Subtask f has to start by 18, so d's completion becomes 17,18, and its start becomes 8,9. The next subtask to be processed will be e. Subtask e has g and i as successors. Subtask g's latest start time is 19 and i's is 22, so subtask e becomes 10,14 for start times and 15,19 for completion times. The last subtask to be processed is a. It has successors c and d. Subtask a has to complete by 9, so the completion time will be 8,9, and its start time will be 0,1. Table 4-3 summarizes the results.

Table 4-3 Subtasks with Slack Time

Subtask ID	Start Time	Completion Time	Critical Path
a	0,1	8,9	
b	0	10	*
c	10	18	*
d	8,9	17,18	
e	10,14	15,19	
f	18	21	*
g	17,19	19,21	
h	21	25	*
i	21,22	24,25	

EXAMPLE 4.7 USING MICROSOFT PROJECT

Open MS Project (version 98). Select PERT view on left menu. Under the Insert pull-down menu, insert a new task. Use the right mouse button to open task information. Change the time for the task to 5 days. Drag from this task to create a new task with a dependency on the first task, or go to the Insert menu to insert another new task. Create the tasks and dependencies from Example 4.5. The tasks on the critical path will be shown in red. Use the left menu bar to see the Gannt chart view of this project.

4.4 Software Cost Estimation

The task of software cost estimation is to determine how many resources are needed to complete the project. Usually this estimate is in programmer-months (PM).

There are two very different approaches to cost estimation. The older approach is called *LOC estimation*, since it is based on initially estimating the number of lines of code that will need to be developed for the project. The newer approach is based on counting function points in the project description.

4.4.1 ESTIMATION OF LINES OF CODE (LOC)

The first step in LOC-based estimation is to estimate the number of lines of code in the finished project. This can be done based on experience, size of previous projects, size of a competitor's solution, or by breaking down the project into smaller pieces and then estimating the size of each of the smaller pieces. A standard approach is, for each piece$_i$, to estimate the maximum possible size, max$_i$, the minimum possible size, min$_i$, and the "best guess" size, best$_i$. The estimate for the whole project is 1/6 of the sum of the maximums, the minimums, and 4 times the best guess:

$$\text{Standard deviation of S} = (sd^2 + sd^2 + \ldots + sd^2)^{1/2}$$
$$\text{Standard deviation of E(i)} = (max - min)/6$$

EXAMPLE 4.8
Team WRT had identified seven subpieces to their project. These are shown in Table 4-4 with their estimates of the size of each subpiece.

Table 4-4   Subpiece Size Estimate (in LOC)

Part	Max Size	Best Guess	Min Size
1	20	30	50
2	10	15	25
3	25	30	45
4	30	35	40
5	15	20	25
6	10	12	14
7	20	22	25

The estimates for each section are as follows:

p1(20 + 4 * 30 + 50)/6 = 190/6 = 31.6
p2(10 + 4 * 15 + 25)/6 = 95/6 = 15.8
p3(25 + 4 * 30 + 45)/6 = 190/6 = 31.6
p4(30 + 4 * 35 + 40)/6 = 220/6 = 36.7
p5(15 + 4 * 20 + 25)/6 = 120/6 = 20
p6(10 + 4 * 12 + 14)/6 = 72/6 = 12
p7(20 + 4 * 22 + 25)/6 = 133/6 = 22.17

The estimate for the whole project is the sum of the estimates for each section:

Whole = 31.6 + 15.8 + 31.6 + 36.7 + 20 + 12 + 22.17 = 170.07 LOC

The estimate for the standard deviation of the estimate is as follows:

$$\text{Standard deviation} = ((50 - 20)^2 + (25 - 10)^2 + (45 - 25)^2$$
$$+ (40 - 30)^2 + (25 - 15)^2 + (14 - 10)^2 + (25 - 20)^2)^{.5}$$
$$= (900 + 225 + 400 + 100 + 100 + 16 + 25)^{.5}$$
$$= 1766^{.5} = 42.03$$

4.4.2   LOC-BASED COST ESTIMATION

The basic LOC approach is a formula that matches the historical data. The basic formula has three parameters:

$$\text{Cost} = \alpha * \text{KLOC}^\beta + \gamma$$

Alpha, α, is the marginal cost per KLOC (thousand lines of code). This is the added cost for an additional thousand lines of code. The parameter beta, β, is an exponent that reflects the nonlinearity of the relationship. A value of beta greater than 1 means that the cost per KLOC increases as the size of the project increases. This is a diseconomy of scale. A value of beta less than 1 reflects an economy of scale. Some studies have found betas greater than 1, and other studies have betas less than 1. The parameter gamma, γ, reflects the fixed cost of doing any project. Studies have found both positive gammas and zero gammas.

EXAMPLE 4.9

Company LMN has recorded the following data from previous projects. Estimate what the parameters for the cost estimation formula should be and how much effort a new project of 30 KLOC should take (see Table 4-5).

Table 4-5   Historical Data

Proj. ID	Size (KLOC)	Effort (PM)
1	50	120
2	80	192
3	40	96
4	10	24
5	20	48

Analyzing or plotting this data would show a linear relationship between size and effort. The slope of the line is 2.4. This would be alpha, α, in the LOC-based cost estimation formula. Since the line is straight (linear relationship), the beta, β, is 1. The gamma, γ, value would be zero.

4.4.3 CONSTRUCTIVE COST MODEL (COCOMO)

COCOMO is the classic LOC cost-estimation formula. It was created by Barry Boehm in the 1970s. He used thousand delivered source instructions (KDSI) as his unit of size. KLOC is equivalent. His unit of effort is the programmer-month (PM).

Boehm divided the historical project data into three types of projects:

1. Application (separate, organic, e.g., data processing, scientific)
2. Utility programs (semidetached, e.g., compilers, linkers, analyzers)
3. System programs (embedded)

He determined the values of the parameters for the cost model for determining effort:

1. Application programs: $PM = 2.4 * (KDSI)^{1.05}$
2. Utility programs: $PM = 3.0 * (KDSI)^{1.12}$
3. Systems programs: $PM = 3.6 * (KDSI)^{1.20}$

EXAMPLE 4.10
Calculate the programmer effort for projects from 5 to 50 KDSI (see Table 4-6)

Table 4-6   COCOMO Effort

Size	Appl	Util	Sys
5K	13.0	18.2	24.8
10K	26.9	39.5	57.1
15K	41.2	62.2	92.8
20K	55.8	86.0	131.1
25K	70.5	110.4	171.3
30K	85.3	135.3	213.2
35K	100.3	160.8	256.6
40K	115.4	186.8	301.1
45K	130.6	213.2	346.9
50K	145.9	239.9	393.6

Boehm also determined that in his project data, there was a standard development time based on the type of project and the size of the project. The following are the formulas for development time (TDEV) in programmer-months:

1. Application programs: $TDEV = 2.5 * (PM)^{0.38}$
2. Utility programs: $TDEV = 2.5 * (PM)^{0.35}$
3. Systems programs: $TDEV = 2.5 * (PM)^{0.32}$

EXAMPLE 4.11

Calculate the standard TDEV using the COCOMO formulas for projects from 5 to 50 KDSI (see Table 4-7).

**Table 4-7 COCOMO
Development Time**

Size	Appl	Util	Sys
5K	6.63	6.90	6.99
10K	8.74	9.06	9.12
15K	10.27	10.62	10.66
20K	11.52	11.88	11.90
25K	12.60	12.97	12.96
30K	13.55	13.93	13.91
35K	14.40	14.80	14.75
40K	15.19	15.59	15.53
45K	15.92	16.33	16.25
50K	16.61	17.02	16.92

4.4.4   FUNCTION POINT ANALYSIS

The idea of function points is to identify and quantify the functionality required for the project. The idea is to count things in the external behavior that will require processing. The classic items to count are as follows:

Inputs
Outputs
Inquiries
Internal files
External interfaces

Inquiries are request-response pairs that do not change the internal data. For example, a request for the address of a specified employee is an inquiry. The whole sequence of asking, supplying the name, and getting the address would count as one inquiry.

Inputs are items of application data that is supplied to the program. The logical input is usually considered one item and individual fields are not usually counted separately. For example, the input of personal data for an employee might be considered one input.

Outputs are displays of application data. This could be a report, a screen display, or an error message. Again, individual fields are usually not considered separate outputs. If the report has multiple lines, for instance, a line for each employee in the department, these lines would all be counted as one output. However, some authorities would count summary lines as separate outputs.

Internal files are the logical files that the customer understands must be maintained by the system. If an actual file contained 1000 entries of personnel data, it would probably be counted as one file. However, if the file contained personnel data, department summary data, and other department data, it would probably be counted as three separate files for the purposes of counting function points.

External interfaces are data that is shared with other programs. For example, the personnel file might be used by human resources for promotion and for payroll. Thus, it would be considered an interface in both systems.

4.4.4.1 Counting Unadjusted Function Points

The individual function point items are identified and then classified as simple, average, or complex. The weights from Table 4-8 are then assigned to each item and the total is summed. This total is called the *unadjusted function points*.

There is no standard for counting function points. Books have been written with different counting rules. The important thing to remember is that function points are trying to measure the amount of effort that will be needed to develop the software. Thus, things that are related to substantial effort need to generate more function points than things that will take little effort. For example, one difference between approaches to counting function points is related to summary lines at the bottom of reports. Some software engineers feel that a summary line means another output should be counted, while others would only count the main items in the report. The answer should be based on how much additional effort that summary line would require.

Specific rules are not as important as consistency within the organization. Working together and reviewing other function point analyses will help build that consistency. Additionally, reviewing the estimate after completion of the project might help determine which items took more effort than indicated by the function point analysis and perhaps which items were overcounted in terms of function points and did not take as much effort as indicated.

Note: Try to make your function points consistent with effort necessary for processing each item.

Table 4-8 Function Point Weights

	Simple	Average	Complex
Outputs	4	5	7
Inquiries	3	4	6
Inputs	3	4	6
Files	7	10	15
Interfaces	5	7	10

EXAMPLE 4.12

The department wants a program that assigns times and rooms for each section and creates a line schedule for the courses. The department has a list of sections with the name of the assigned professor and the anticipated size. The department also has a list of rooms with the maximum number of students each room will hold There are also sets of classes that cannot be taught at the same time. Additionally, professors cannot teach two courses at the same time.

This program is much more difficult than the complexity of the inputs and outputs. It has two main inputs: the file with the list of sections, assigned professor, and anticipated size, and the file with the list of rooms with the maximum size. These two files, although simple to read, will be difficult to process, so they will be rated complex. There will be an additional file with the sets of classes that cannot be taught at the same time. Again, this file is simple in structure but will be difficult to process. The last line has a restriction that is not an input or output.

There is an output, the line schedule. This is a complex output. There are no inquiries or interfaces mentioned, nor any mention about files being maintained.

4.4.5 PRODUCTIVITY

One of the important measures is the productivity of the software developers. This is determined by dividing the total size of the finished product by the total effort of all the programmers. This has units of LOC/programmer-day. An alternative is to measure the productivity in terms of function points per programmer-day.

Note that productivity includes all the effort spent in all phases of the software life cycle.

EXAMPLE 4.13

Company XYZ spent the following effort for each life cycle phase of the latest project (see Table 4-9). Calculate the effort in terms of LOC/programmer-day and in terms of function points/programmer day. The function point estimate was 50 unadjusted function points. The finished project included 950 lines of code.

Table 4-9 Effort During Phases

Phase	Programmer-Days
Requirements	20
Design	10
Implementation	10
Testing	15
Documentation	10

The total effort was 65 programmer-days. This gives a productivity of 950/65 = 14.6 lines of code/programmer-days. Using unadjusted function points (fp), the productivity is 50 fp/65 days = 0.77 fp/programmer-days.

4.4.6 EVALUATING ESTIMATIONS

To evaluate estimations, a measure needs to be calculated. Tom DeMarco proposed the *estimate quality factor* (EQF). DeMarco defines the EQF as the area under the actual curve divided by area between the estimate and the actual value. This is the inverse of the percentage error or the mean relative error. Thus, the higher the EQF, the better was the series of estimates. DeMarco said that values over 8 are reasonable.

EXAMPLE 4.11
The following estimates were given for a project that cost 3.5 million dollars when it was completed after 11.5 months:

Initial	1.5 months	5.5 months	8 months
2.3 million	3.1 million	3.9 million	3.4 million

The total area is 11.5 months times 3.5 million = 40.25 million month-dollars. The difference between the actual curve and the estimate is $|2.3 - 3.5| * 1.5 + |3.1 - 3.5| * 4 + |3.9 - 3.5| * 2.5 + |3.4 - 3.5| * 3.5 = 4.75$ million month-dollars. The ratio is 40.25/4.75 = 8.7.

4.4.7 AUTOMATED ESTIMATION TOOLS

Numerous tools are available on the Internet that will calculate COCOMO or COCOMO2. Most have very simple interfaces. Search for COCOMO using any browser, and it should find multiple sites.[1]

Review Questions

1. What is the distinction between a WBS and a process model?
2. Why should a WBS be a tree?
3. What happens when there is not a completion criterion for a task in a WBS?
4. What is the advantage of using a PERT diagram?
5. Why does delaying a task on the critical path delay the whole project?
6. Is the critical path important if only one person is working on a project?
7. What is the importance of slack time?
8. Why is slack time based on the earliest time of the latest start times of successor tasks?
9. Draw a diagram that shows economy of scale and diseconomy of scale. Label the diagram and explain which is which.
10. It is very common to use the default version of estimation. Consider the last time someone asked you to give an estimate of anything. Was the estimate you gave the default definition of an estimate or DeMarco's proposed definition of an estimate?
11. Why should the parameters for cost estimation be determined from a company's data?

Problems

1. Create a WBS for the task of painting a room. Assume that the process model is for home work projects with activities: plan work, buy supplies, do work, clean up.

---

[1] A couple of useful sites are sunset.usc.edu/research/COCOMOII or www.jsc.nasa.gov/bu2/COCOMO.html.

2. Create a WBS for the software development of the software for the following dental office:

> Tom is starting a dental practice in a small town. He will have a dental assistant, a dental hygienist, and a receptionist. He wants a system to manage the appointments.
>
> When a patient calls for an appointment, the receptionist will check the calendar and will try to schedule the patient as early as possible to fill in vacancies. If the patient is happy with the proposed appointment, the receptionist will enter the appointment with the patient name and purpose of appointment. The system will verify the patient name and supply necessary details from the patient records, including the patient's ID number. After each exam or cleaning, the hygienist or assistant will mark the appointment as completed, add comments, and then schedule the patient for the next visit if appropriate.
>
> The system will answer queries by patient name and by date. Supporting details from the patient's records are displayed along with the appointment information. The receptionist can cancel appointments. The receptionist can print out a notification list for making reminder calls 2 days before appointments. The system includes the patient's phone numbers from the patient records. The receptionist can also print out daily and weekly work schedules with all the patients.

3. Create a WBS for the software development of the software for the following B&B problem:

> Tom and Sue are starting a bed-and-breakfast in a small New England town. They will have three bedrooms for guests. They want a system to manage the reservations and to monitor expenses and profits. When a potential customer calls for a reservation, they will check the calendar, and if there is a vacancy, they will enter the customer name, address, phone number, dates, agreed upon price, credit card number, and room number(s). Reservations must be guaranteed by 1 day's payment.
>
> Reservations will be held without guarantee for an agreed upon time. If not guaranteed by that date, the reservation will be dropped.

4. Create a WBS for the software development of the software for the following automobile dealership problem:

> An automobile dealer wants to automate its inventory. It can record all of the cars that a customer purchases. It records all repairs. It records all arriving shipments of repair parts. The dealer wants daily reports on total daily repairs, daily sales, and total inventory. This report is called "dailyreport." The dealer also keeps track of all customers and potential customers that visit the dealership. The dealer also wants a monthly report showing all visits and purchases by customers listed by day of the month. The dealer also wants the ability to query about any customer or potential customer.

5. Draw the PERT diagram for the tasks of Problem 1.

6. Draw the PERT diagram for the given set of tasks and dependencies. Complete the table showing the critical path and the slack times.

Node	Dep	Time	Start	Finish
a		10		
b	a	5		
c	a	2		
d	a	3		
e	b,c	7		
f	b,d	9		
g	c,d	5		
h	e,f,g	6		

7. Draw the PERT diagrams for the given set of tasks and dependencies. Complete the table showing the critical path and the slack times.

Node	Dependencies	Time	Start Time	Stop Time
a		10		
b	e	10		
c	d,f	10		
d	a,f,b	20		
e	a,f	8		
f	a	5		

8. Estimate the cost parameters from the given set of data:

Project	Size (KLOC)	Cost (programmer-months)
a	30	84
b	5	14
c	20	56

d	50	140
e	100	280
f	10	28

9. Estimate the cost parameters from the given set of data:

Project	Size (KLOC)	Cost (programmer-months)
a	30	95
b	5	80
c	20	65
d	50	155
e	100	305
f	10	35

10. Calculate COCOMO effort, TDEV, average staffing, and productivity for an organic project that is estimated to be 39,800 lines of code.

11. Calculate the unadjusted function points for the problem description of Problem 2.

Answers to Review Questions

1. What is the distinction between a WBS and a process model?

A process model describes the software activities in a generic sense, that is, for many different projects. It describes the process, the artifacts produced and used, and the actors responsible for the activities. A process model is a graph; it can have cycles and so on. A work breakdown structure is a tree that expands the process model's activities with details and necessary subtasks that are specific for a particular project. A WBS task that appears in every project should also be in the process model.

2. Why should a WBS be a tree?

If there are loops in a WBS, it means that some task recursively depends on itself, which is impossible. A loop will normally happen when some task is not defined properly. If there are two paths to a task, it normally means that two different higher-level tasks depend on that common subtask. It only needs to be shown (and done) once.

3. What happens when there is not a completion criterion for a task in a WBS?

It means that it will not be clear if progress is being made or when it is done. It also may mean that it is not clear what actually needs to be done. For example, a subtask such as "research XXX" is not well specified. There should be a goal to the research and that should be clearly stated in the task description.

4. What is the advantage of using a PERT diagram?

Although the WBS will develop a list of tasks, it may be difficult to see which tasks have to be done first and which tasks will determine the final completion time. These tasks are on the critical path.

5. Why does delaying a task on the critical path delay the whole project?

The critical path is defined as the set of tasks that determine the minimum time for completing the project. Practically, if a task is on the critical path and it is delayed, that means the start time and ending time of the next task on the critical path will be delayed. This will ripple down to the last task on the critical path, and the project will be delayed.

6. Is the critical path important if only one person is working on a project?

It is important only if all tasks are on the critical path. If there are tasks not on the critical path and those tasks cannot be done in parallel since there is only one person, the time required for those tasks will have the be added to the time of the critical path to determine the completion time.

7. What is the importance of slack time?

Although tasks not on the critical path do not determine the minimal completion time, if those tasks are not done in a timely fashion, the completion time will be delayed. The slack time shows the range of time in which that task must be completed.

8. Why is slack time based on the earliest of the latest start times of the successor tasks?

Slack time is based on the earliest such start time because if that task was delayed past that start time, that task would not be completed in time and the ripple effect would delay the whole project.

9. Draw a diagram that shows economy of scale and diseconomy of scale. Label the diagram and explain which is which.

A line that curves upward shows a diseconomy of scale. That is, with bigger projects, the cost per unit of size increases. A line that curves downward shows an economy of scale. That is, the bigger the project, the cheaper the cost per unit of size. See Fig. 4-4.

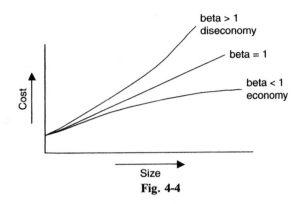

Fig. 4-4

10. It is very common to use the default version of estimation. Consider the last time someone asked you to give an estimate of anything. Was the estimate you gave the default definition of an estimate or DeMarco's proposed definition of an estimate?

When my students ask when an assignment will be graded, I too often give the time it would take if I did not have any other tasks to do and I was not interrupted. That answer is not realistic because there are always more pressing tasks and interruptions.

11. Why should the parameters for cost estimation be determined from a company's data?

Each company has different practices, standards, policies, and types of software that it develops. It is unrealistic to expect that the parameters found to be good predictors by large defense contractors should be the same as those for small, in-house development projects.

Answers to Problems

1. Create a WBS for painting a room.

(Process model activities are not shown.)

a. Select color for room	Color decided
b. Buy paint	Cans of paint
c. Buy brushes	Brushes
d. Prepare walls	Clean walls
e. Open paint cans	Opened cans
f. Stir paint	Stirred paint
g. Paint walls	Painted walls
h. Clean up	Cleaned and painted walls

2. Create a WBS for the dental office problem.

(The life cycle phases and the PM activities have been left off.)

Develop risk assessment	Assessment spec
Estimate effort	Cost estimate
Plan schedule	Schedule
Review risks, estimation, and schedule with dentist	Dentist's approval
Design object model	Object model
Review object model with dentist	Dentist's approval
Get specs of patient records system	Specs
Develop prototype interface with patient records	Working prototype
Review form of reminder list with receptionist and dentist	Dentist's approval
Review form of daily and weekly schedule with dental staff	Dentist's approval
Review design of class model with team	Review document
Implement	Compiled code
Unit test successfully with C0 coverage	Test report
Integrate system	Compiled code
System test	Test report
Training and alpha testing in dental office	Test report
Review system with dental staff	Dentist's approval
Acceptance test by staff	Dentist's approval
Deliver user manual and documentation	Manuals delivered

3. Create a WBS for the B&B problem.

(The PM activities and the deliverables have been left off.)

Feasibility Analysis
    Discuss Web-based options with Tom and Sue.
    Determine if Web-based or stand-alone system.
Requirements
    Elicit requirements from Tom and Sue.
    Build requirements document.
    Review requirements with Tom and Sue.
Design
    Design prototype reservation system.
    Design expense and profit section.
Implementation
    Build prototype reservation system.
    Implement expense and profit section.
Testing
    Test prototype.
    Test expense and profit section.
Delivery
    Review prototype with Tom and Sue.
    Review total system with Tom and Sue.

4. Create a WBS for the automobile dealership problem.

(The life cycle phases and the PM activities have been left off.)

Requirements
   Elicit requirements from dealer.
   Build requirements document.
   Review requirements with dealer.
   Create preliminary user manual.
   Review preliminary user manual.
   Build test cases.
Design
   Design prototype automobile system.
   Design format for reports.
Implementation
   Build prototype automobile system.
   Implement queries and reports section.
   Review prototype with dealer.
   Implement final version.
Testing
   Test final version at dealership.
Delivery
   Train staff
   Deliver documentation.

5. Draw a PERT diagram for painting a room:

The PERT diagram is shown in Fig. 4-5.

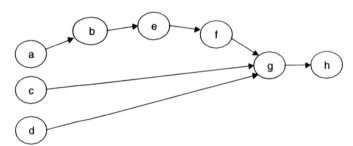

Fig. 4-5.   PERT diagram for painting.

6. Draw a PERT diagram and complete the table.

(Critical path indicated with asterisks in table.) See also Fig. 4-6.

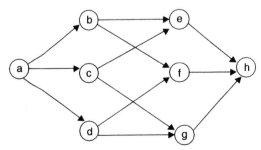

Fig. 4-6.   PERT diagram.

Node	Dep	Time	Start	Finish
a		10	0	10*
b	a	5	10	15*
c	a	2	10,24	12,26
d	a	3	10,21	13,24
e	b,c	7	12,26	19,33
f	b,d	9	24	33*
g	c,d	5	13,28	18,33
h	e,f,g	6	33	39*

7. Draw a PERT diagram and complete the table for the given set of tasks and dependencies.

Node	Dependencies	Time	Start Time	Stop Time
a		10	0	10
b	e	10	23	33
c	d,f	10	53	63
d	a,f,b	20	33	53
e	a,f	8	15	23
f	a	5	10	15

Everything is on critical path; no slack times. See Fig. 4-7.

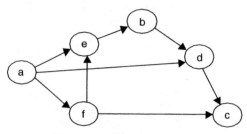

Fig. 4-7.   PERT diagram

8. Estimate the cost parameters from the given set of data.

   Cost = 3.8 * Size (**KLOC**)

9. Estimate the cost parameters from the given set of data.

   Cost = 4.0 * Size (**KLOC**) + 5.0

10. Calculate COCOMO effort, TDEV, average staffing, and productivity for an organic project that is estimated to be 39,800 lines of code.

    An organic project uses the application formulas. Cost = $2.4 * (KDSI)^{1.05}$
    Cost = $2.4 * 39.8^{1.05}$ = 2.4 * 47.85 = 114.8 programmer-months
    TDEV = $2.5 * (PM)^{0.38}$ = 2.5 * 6.06 = 15.15 months
    Average staffing = Cost/TDEV = 114.8/15.15 = 7.6 programmers
    Productivity = 39,800 **LOC**/(114.8 PM * 20 days/month) = 17.3 LOC/programmer-day

11. Calculate the unadjusted function points for the problem description of Problem 2.

Type	Simple	Average	Complex	Total
Inputs	Patient name Appt completed Appt purpose	Cancel appt		13
Outputs	Comments	Calendar Supporting details Appt information Notification list	Daily schedule Weekly schedule	38
Inquires	Query by name Query by date	Verify patient Check calendar Available appt		18
Files		Patient data		10
Interfaces				
Total				79

CHAPTER 5

Software Metrics

5.1   Introduction

Science is based on measurement. Improving a process requires understanding of the numerical relationships. This requires measurement.

Software measurement is the mapping of symbols to objects. The purpose is to quantify some attribute of the objects, for example, to measure the size of software projects. Additionally, a purpose may be to predict some other attribute that is not currently measurable, such as effort needed to develop a software project.

Not all mappings of symbols to objects are useful. An important concern is the validation of metrics. However, validation is related to the use of the metric. An example is a person's height. Height is useful for predicting the ability of a person to pass through a doorway without hitting his or her head. Just having a high correlation between a measure and an attribute is not sufficient to validate a measure. For example, a person's shoe size is highly correlated to the person's height. However, shoe size is normally not acceptable as a measure of a person's height.

The following are criteria for valid metrics[1]:

1. A metric must allow different entities to be distinguished.
2. A metric must obey a representation condition.
3. Each unit of the attribute must contribute an equivalent amount to the metric.
4. Different entities can have the same attribute value.

Many times, the attribute of interest is not directly measurable. In this case, an *indirect measure* is used. An indirect measure involves a measure and a prediction formula. For example, density is not a direct measure. It is calculated from mass and density, which are both direct measures. In computer science, many of the

[1] R. Harrison, S. Counsell, R. Nithi. "An Evaluation of the MOOD Set of Object-oriented Software Metrics." IEEE TOSE 24:6, June 1998, 491–496.

"ilities" (maintainability, readability, testability, quality, complexity, etc.) cannot be measured directly, and indirect measures for these attributes are the goal of many metrics programs.

The following are criteria for valid indirect metrics:

1. The model must be explicitly defined.
2. The model must be dimensionally consistent.
3. There should be no unexpected discontinuities.
4. Units and scale types must be correct.

5.2 Software Measurement Theory

The representational theory of measurement has been studied for over 100 years. It involves an empirical relation system, a numerical relation system, and a relation-preserving mapping between the two systems.

The empirical relation system (E, R) consists of two parts:

- A set of entities, E
- A set of relationships, R

The relationship is usually "less than or equal." Note that not everything has to be related. That is, the set R may be a partial order.[2]

The numerical relation system (N, P) also consists of two parts:

- A set of entities, N. Also called the "answer set," this set is usually numbers— natural numbers, integers, or reals.
- A set of relations, P. This set usually already exists and is often "less than" or "less than or equal."

The relation-preserving mapping, M, maps (E, R) to (N, P). The important restriction on this mapping is called the ***representation condition***. There are two possible representation conditions. The most restrictive version says that if two entities are related in either system, then the images (or pre-images) in the other system are related:

$$x \text{ rel } y \text{ iff } M(x) \text{ rel } M(y)^3$$

The less restrictive version says that if two entities are related in the empirical system, then the images of those two entities in the numerical system are related in the same way:

$$M(x) \text{ rel } M(y) \text{ if } x \text{ rel } y$$

---

[2] A partial order is strictly defined as an order that satisfies three axioms: every element is related to itself, the relation cannot hold both ways between two elements, and transitivity. It is not required to be total. That is, not every two elements are related.

[3] "x is related to y if and only if the mapping of x is related to the mapping of y."

Classical measurement theory authors have used both versions. The advantage of the second version is that partial orders in the empirical system can be mapped to integers or reals that are both totally ordered.

EXAMPLE 5.1   HEIGHT OF PEOPLE
The classic example of mapping an empirical system to a numerical system is the height of people. In the empirical system, there is a well-understood height relationship among people. Given two people who are standing next to each other, everyone would agree about who is taller. This is the empirical system: people are the entities and the well-understood relation is "shorter or the same height."

The numerical system is the real number system (either metric or imperial units) with the standard relation of less than or equal.

The mapping is just the standard measured height of people. This is usually measured barefoot, standing straight against a wall.

The representation condition (either version) is satisfied, since if Fred is shorter than or equal to Bill, then Fred's measured height is less than or equal to Bill's measured height.

EXAMPLE 5.2
Develop a measure, BIG, for people that combines both weight and height.

Empirically, if two people are the same height, the heavier is bigger, and if two people are the same weight, the taller is bigger. If we use this notion, we can have a partial order that most people would agree with. The only pair of persons that we would not order by this would be if one was heavier and the other was taller.

Numerically, we can use a tuple, < height, weight >. Each part of the tuple would be a real number. Two tuples would be related if both parts were related in the same direction. That is, if x, y are tuples, than x is less than or equal to y in "bigness" if $x_{height} =< y_{height}$ and $x_{weight} =< y_{weight}$. This is also a partial order, and both versions of the representation condition are satisfied.

5.2.1   MONOTONICITY

An important characteristic of a measure is ***monotonicity***. It means that the value of the measure of an attribute does not change direction as the attribute increases in the object. For example, the count of lines of code will not decrease as more code is added.

EXAMPLE 5.3
A linear function is monotonic, since it always goes in the same direction. A quadratic function is usually not monotonic. For example, $y = 5x - x^2$ is not monotonic in the range $x = 0$ to $x = 10$. From $x = 0$ to $x = 5$, y increases. From $x = 5$ to $x = 10$, y decreases.

5.2.2   MEASUREMENT SCALES

There are five different scale types: nominal, ordinal, interval, ratio, and absolute.

The least restrictive measurement is using the ***nominal*** scale type. This type basically assigns numbers or symbols without regard to any quantity. The classic example for a nominal scale measure is the numbers on sports uniforms. We do not think that one player is better than another just because the number on one uniform is bigger or smaller than the number on the other uniform. There is no formula for converting from one nominal scale measure to another nominal scale measure.

In an *ordinal* scale measure, there is an implied ordering of the entities by the numbers assigned to the entity. The classic example is class rank. If a student is ranked first, her performance has been better than a student who is ranked second, or third, or any other number greater than 1. However, we never assume that the numerical difference in rank is significant. That is, we don't assume that the difference between the first and second student is the same as the difference between the 100th and 101st student. Any formula that converts from one ordinal scale measure to another ordinal scale measure for the same entity must preserve the ordering.

In an *interval* scale measure, the amount of the difference is constant. An example is temperature. There are two instances of temperature measures that are commonly used, Fahrenheit and Celsius. The formula for converting from a Celsius scale measure to a Fahrenheit scale measure is $9/5 * x + 32$. With any two interval scale measures for the same attribute, the formula for conversion must be of the form $ax + b$.

In a *ratio* scale measure, the amount of the difference is constant and there is a well-understood zero that any scale measure would use. For example, money, length, and height are measurements using ratio scales. These measurements have well-understood notions of zero: zero money, zero height, and zero length. Any formula for converting from one set of units to another—from centimeters to inches, for example—would just use a multiplicative constant.

The *absolute* is a counting scale measure. The units are obvious and well understood. Counting marbles is an example of an absolute scale measure.

5.2.3 STATISTICS

Not all statistics are appropriate for all scales. The following indicates which common statistical methods are appropriate:

Nominal scale: Only mode, median, and percentiles
Ordinal scale: The above and Spearman correlations
Interval scale: The above and mean, standard deviation, and Pearson correlations
Ratio scale: All statistics
Absolute scale: All statistics

EXAMPLE 5.4 AVERAGES
Temperature is an interval scale measure. Thus, it makes statistical sense to give an average temperature. However, the numbers on baseball players' uniforms are a nominal scale measure. It does not make sense to give the average of the numbers on a team's uniforms. Similarly, the average ranking of the students in a class or the average of a student's rankings in a number of classes is not appropriate.

5.3   Product Metrics

Product metrics are metrics that can be calculated from the document independent of how it was produced. Generally, these are concerned with the structure of the source code. Product metrics could be defined for other documents. For example, the number of paragraphs in a requirements specification would be a product metric.

> **EXAMPLE 5.5   LINES OF CODE**
> The most basic metric for size is the *lines of code metric*. There are many different ways to count lines of code. The definition may be a simple as the number of NEW LINE characters in the file. Often comments are excluded from the count of lines. Sometimes blank lines or lines with only delimiters are excluded. Sometimes statements are counted instead of lines.

5.3.1   McCABE'S CYCLOMATIC NUMBER

McCabe's cyclomatic number, introduced in 1976, is, after lines of code, one of the most commonly used metrics in software development. Also called "McCabe's complexity measure" from the title of the original journal article, it is based on graph theory's cyclomatic number. McCabe tries to measure the complexity of a program. The premise is that complexity is related to the control flow of the program. Graph theory uses a formula, $C = e - n + 1$ to calculate the cyclomatic number. McCabe uses the slightly modified formula:

$$C = e - n + 2p$$

where:

e = Number of edges
n = Number of nodes
p = Number of strongly connected components (which is normally 1)

> **EXAMPLE 5.6**
> Determine the cyclomatic number from the control flow graph shown in Fig. 5-1.
>
>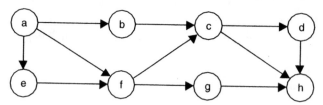
>
> **Fig. 5-1.   Control flow graph.**
>
> There are 8 nodes, so $n = 8$. There are 11 arcs, so $e = 11$. The cyclomatic number is $C = 11 - 8 + 2 = 5$.

A *planar graph* is a graph that can be drawn without lines crossing. The Swiss mathematician Leonhard Euler (1707–1783) proved for planar graphs that

$2 = n - e + r$, where $r =$ number of regions, $e =$ number of edges, and $n =$ number of nodes. A region is an area enclosed (or defined) by arcs. Using algebra, this can be converted to $r = e - n + 2$. Therefore, the number of regions on a planar graph equals the cyclomatic number.

EXAMPLE 5.7
Label the regions in the control flow graph from Example 5.6 with Roman numerals.
    As shown in Fig. 5-2, there are five regions. Region I is the outside of the graph.

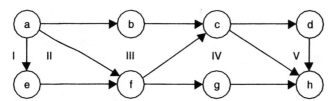

Fig. 5-2.   Control flow graph with roman numerals.

Calculating the cyclomatic number from control flow graphs is time-consuming. Constructing a control flow graph from a large program would be prohibitively time-consuming. McCabe found a more direct method of calculating his measure. He found that the number of regions is usually equal to one more than the number of decisions in a program, $C = \pi + 1$, where π is the number of decisions.

    In source code, an IF statement, a WHILE loop, or a FOR loop is considered one decision. A CASE statement or other multiple branch is counted as one less decision than the number of possible branches.

    Control flow graphs are required to have a distinct starting node and a distinct stopping node. If this is violated, the number of decisions will not be one less than the number of regions.

EXAMPLE 5.8
Label the decisions in the control flow graph of Example 5.6 with lowercase letters.
    As shown in Fig. 5-3, from node a, there are three arcs, so there must be two decisions, labeled a and b. From nodes c and f, there are two arcs and so one decision each. The other nodes have at most one exit and so no decisions. There are four decisions, so $C = 4 + 1 = 5$.

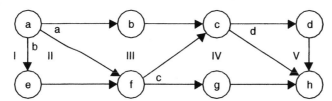

Fig. 5-3.   Control flow graph with lowercase letters.

EXAMPLE 5.9

Calculate the cyclomatic number using the invalid control flow graph shown in Fig. 5-4.

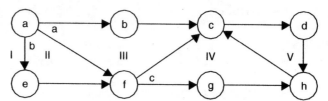

Fig. 5-4.   Invalid control flow graph.

The cfg is the same as earlier examples, except that the c-h arc has been replaced by an h-c arc. This will not change the counts of nodes, edges, or regions. Thus, the first two methods of counting the cyclomatic number will not change. However, decision d has been eliminated, so the third method will not give the same answer. However, this is not a valid cfg, since there is now no stopping node.

Threshold Value

An important aspect of a metric is guidance about when the values are reasonable and when the values are not reasonable. McCabe analyzed a large project and discovered that for modules with cyclomatic number over 10, the modules had histories of many more errors and many more difficulties in maintenance. Thus, 10 has been accepted as the threshold value for the cyclomatic number in a module. If the cyclomatic number is greater than 10, efforts should be made to reduce the value or to split the module.

5.3.2   HALSTEAD'S SOFTWARE SCIENCE

Maurice Halstead was one of the first researchers in software metrics. He did his work in the late 1960s and 1970s. His goal was to identify what contributed to the complexity in software. He empirically looked for measures of intrinsic size. After finding what he felt were good measures and prediction formulas, he tried to develop a coherent theory. His simple metrics are still considered valid, while his more complex metrics and prediction formulas have been found to be suspect.

Basic Entities—Operators and Operands

The basic approach that gave Halstead good results was to consider any program to be a collection of tokens, which he classified as either operators or operands. *Operands* were tokens that had a value. Typically, variables and constants were operands. Everything else was considered an *operator*. Thus, commas, parentheses, arithmetic operators, brackets, and so forth were all considered operators.

All tokens that always appear as a pair, triple, and so on will be counted together as one token. For example, a left parenthesis and a right parenthesis will be considered as one occurrence of the token parenthesis. A language that has an if-then construction will be considered to have an if-then token.

Halstead also was concerned about algorithms and not about declarations, i/o statements, and so on. Thus, he did not count declarations, input or output statements, or comments. However, currently most organizations would count all parts of a program.

Halstead's definitions of operator and operand are open to many interpretations. No standard has been accepted for deciding ambiguous situations. The good news is that as long as an organization is consistent, it doesn't matter. The bad news is that people in one organization cannot compare their results with the results from other organizations.

The author recommends a syntax-based approach where all operands are user-defined tokens and all operators are the tokens defined by the syntax of the language.

Basic Measures—η_1 and η_2

The count of unique operators in a program is η_1 (pronounced "eta one"), and the count of unique operands in a program is η_2 (pronounced "eta two").

The total count of unique tokens is $\eta = \eta_1 + \eta_2$. This is the basic measure of the size of the program.

> **EXAMPLE 5.10**
> Identify the unique operators and operands in the following code that does multiplication by repeated addition.
>
> ```
> Z = 0;
> while X > 0
>         Z = Z + Y ;
>         X = X-1 ;
> end-while ;
> print(Z) ;
> ```
>
> operators
> ```
>   = ; while-endwhile > +-print ()
> ```
>
> operands
> ```
>   Z 0 X Y 1
> ```
>
> thus, $\eta_1 = 8$ and $\eta_2 = 5$

Potential Operands, $\eta_2{}^*$

Halstead wanted to consider and compare different implementations of algorithms. He developed the concept of potential operands that represents the minimal set of values needed for any implementation of the given algorithm. This is usually calculated by counting all the values that are not initially set within the algorithm. It will include values read in, parameters passed in, and global values accessed within the algorithm.

Length, N

The next basic measure is total count of operators, N_1, and the total count of operands, N_2. These are summed to get the length of the program in tokens:

$$N = N_1 + N_2$$

EXAMPLE 5.11
Calculate Halstead's length for the code of Example 5.10.

operators

=	3
;	5
while-endwhile	1
>	1
+	1
−	1
print	1
( )	1

operands

Z	4
O	2
X	3
Y	2
1	1

There are 14 occurrences of operators, so N_1 is 14. Similarly, N_2 is 12.
$N = N_1 + N_2 = 14 + 12 = 26$.

Estimate of the Length (est N or N_hat)

The estimate of length is the most basic of Halstead's prediction formulas. Based on just an estimate of the number of operators and operands that will be used in a program, this formula allows an estimate of the actual size of the program in terms of tokens:

$$\text{est } N = \eta_1 * \log_2 \eta_1 + \eta_2 * \log_2 \eta_2$$

EXAMPLE 5.12
Calculate the estimated length for the code of Example 5.10.
   The $\log_2$ of x is the exponent to which 2 must be raised to give a result equal to x. So, log2 of 2 is 1, log2 of 4 is 2, of 8 is 3, of 16 is 4:

$$\log_2 \text{ of } \eta_1 = \log_2 8 = 3$$
$$\log_2 \text{ of } \eta_2 = \log_2 5 = 2.32$$
$$\text{est } N = 8 * 3 + 5 * 2.32 = 24 + 11.6 = 35.6$$

while the actual N is 26. This would be considered borderline. It is probably not a bad approximation for such a small program.

From experience, I have found that if N and est N are not within about 30 percent of each other, it may not be reasonable to apply any of the other software science measures.

Volume, V

Halstead thought of volume as a 3D measure, when it is really related to the number of bits it would take to encode the program being measured.[4] In other words:

$$V = N * \log_2(\eta_1 + \eta_2)$$

> **EXAMPLE 5.13**
> Calculate V for the code of Example 5.10.
> $$V = 26 * \log_2 13 = 26 * 3.7 = 96.2$$

The volume gives the number of bits necessary to encode that many different values. This number is hard to interpret.

Potential Volume, V*

The potential volume is the minimal size of a solution to the problem, solved in any language. Halstead assumes that in the minimal implementation, there would only be two operators: the name of the function and a grouping operator. The minimal number of operands is η_2^*.

$$V^* = (2 + \eta_2^*) \log_2(2 + \eta_2^*)$$

Implementation Level, L

Since we have the actual volume and the minimal volume, it is natural to take a ratio. Halstead divides the potential volume by the actual. This relates to how close the current implementation is to the minimal implementation as measured by the potential volume. The implementation level is unitless.

$$L = V^*/V$$

The basic measures described so far are reasonable. Many of the ideas of operands and operators have been used in many other metric efforts. The remaining measures are given for historical interest and are not recommended as being useful or valid.

Effort, E

Halstead wanted to estimate how much time (effort) was needed to implement this algorithm. He used a notion of elementary mental discriminations (emd).

$$E = V/L$$

The units are elementary mental discriminations (emd). Halstead's effort is not monotonic—in other words, there are programs such that if you add statements, the calculated effort decreases.

---

[4] Encoding n different items would require at a minimum $\log_2 n$ bits for each item. To encode a sequence of N, such items would require $N * \log_2 n$.

Time, T

Next, Halstead wanted to estimate the time necessary to implement the algorithm. He used some work developed by a psychologist in the 1950s, John Stroud. Stroud had measured how fast a subject could view items passed rapidly in front of his face. S is the Stroud number (emd/sec) taken from those experiments. Halstead used 18 emd/sec as the value of S.

$$T = E/S$$

5.3.3   HENRY–KAFURA INFORMATION FLOW

Sallie Henry and Dennis Kafura developed a metric to measure the intermodule complexity of source code. The complexity is based on the flow of information into and out of a module. For each module, a count is made of all the information flows into the module, in_i, and all the information flows out of the module, out_i. These information flows include parameter passing, global variables, and inputs and outputs. They also use a measure of the size of each module as a multiplicative factor. LOC and complexity measures have been used as this weight.

$$HK_i = weight_i * (out_i * in_i)^2$$

The total measure is the sum of the HK_i from each module.

EXAMPLE 5.14

Calculate the HK information flow metrics from the following information. Assume the weight of each module is 1.

mod #	a	b	c	d	e	f	g	h
in_i	4	3	1	5	2	5	6	1
out_i	3	3	4	3	4	4	2	6

mod	a	b	c	d	e	f	g	h
HK_i	144	81	16	225	64	400	144	36

HK for the whole program will be 1110.

5.4 Process Metrics

Productivity

Productivity is one of the basic process metrics. It is calculated by dividing the total delivered source lines by the programmer-days attributed to the project. The units are normally LOC/programmer-day. In many projects in the 1960s the productivity was 1 LOC/programmer-day. In large projects, the typical productivity will range from 2 to 20 LOC/programmer-day. In small, individual projects, the productivity can be much higher.

EXAMPLE 5.15
The project totaled 100 KLOC. Twenty programmers worked on the project for a year. This year included the whole effort for the requirements, design, implementation, testing, and delivery phases. Assume that there are about 240 workdays in a year (20 days a month for 12 months, no vacations). The productivity is 100,000 LOC / 20 * 240 days = 20.8 LOC/programmer-day.

5.5 The GQM Approach

Vic Basili and Dieter Rombach developed this approach at the University of Maryland. GQM stands for goals, questions, and metrics. The idea is to first identify the goals of the approach. Next, questions are developed related to these goals. Finally, metrics are developed to measure the attributes related to the questions.

EXAMPLE 5.16
Use the GQM approach for the problem of customer satisfaction.

Goal—Customer satisfaction
Questions—Are customers dissatisfied when problems are found?
Metric—Number of customer defect reports

Review Questions

1. Explain why the height example satisfies the criteria for valid metrics.
2. A study of grade school children found a high correlation between shoe size and reading ability. Does this mean that shoe size is a good measure of intelligence?

3. Explain why money is a ratio scale measure and not just an interval scale.

4. Explain why GPA is not sound by measurement theory.

5. Why is complexity not readily measurable?

6. What is the advantage of having a partial order on the empirical relation system?

7. Why is the number of decisions plus 1 an important method for calculating McCabe's cyclomatic number?

8. Why is monotonicity an important characteristic of a size or effort metric such as Halstead's effort metric?

 **Problems**

1. Identify the proper scale for each of the following measures:

   LOC
   McCabe's cyclomatic number
   Average depth of nesting
   Maximum depth of nesting

2. Show that the temperature scales of Celsius and Fahrenheit are an interval scale using the Celsius temperatures of 20, 30, and 40 degrees.

3. Show that McCabe's cyclomatic number satisfies the representational theory of measurement.

4. Show that McCabe's cyclomatic number is an interval scale measure.

5. Calculate McCabe's cyclomatic number on the following source code. Draw a control flow graph. Label the regions with Roman numerals.

```
read x,y,z;
type = ''scalene'';
if (x == y or x == z or y == z) type =''isosceles'';
if (x == y and x == z) type =''equilateral'';
if (x >= y+z or y >= x+z or z >= x+y) type =''not a triangle'';
if (x <= 0 or y <= 0 or| z <= 0) type =''bad inputs'';
print type;
```

6. Calculate McCabe's cyclomatic number from the control flow graph, shown in Fig. 5-5.

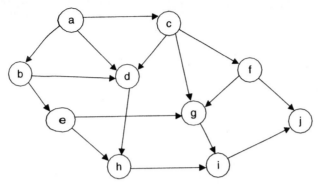

Fig. 5-5.   Control flow graph.

7. Calculate Halstead's basic measures on the triangle code from Problem 5.

8. Calculate Halstead's basic measures on the factorial code given below:

```
int fact (int n) {
        if (n == 0 )
                    { return 1 ; }
        else
                    { return n * fact (n-1) ; }
        }
```

9. Given the following code section, draw the control flow graph and calculate McCabe's cyclomatic number using all three approaches. Show which lines of code are represented by which nodes. On the CFG, label the regions with Roman numerals and the decisions with lowercase letters.

```
cin >> a >> b >> c;
if (a > 10)
{
        cout << ``hello'';
        if (b < a)
        {
                cout << ``part 1'';
                if ( c > a)
                {
                        cout << ``part 2'';
                }
        }
        else
        {
                cout << ``part 3'';
        }
}
cout << ``exiting'';
```

10. In Problem 9, count Halstead's η_1 and η_2. Calculate η and N. Count all strings as occurrences of one operand called "string." Show your work.

Answers to Review Questions

1. Explain why the height example satisfies the criteria for valid metrics.

Criteria 1: Different people can be different heights.
Criteria 2: Any two people that we feel are related in height, their numerical heights would agree.
Criteria 3: Each additional height on a person matches the increase in numerical height.
Criteria 4: Different people can be the same height.

2. A study of grade school children found a high correlation between shoe size and reading ability. Does this mean that shoe size is a good measure of intelligence?

No, shoe size correlates well with age. Age correlates well with reading ability. Neither would be a good measure, since neither would satisfy the representation condition.

3. Explain why is money a ratio scale measure and not just an interval scale.

Money has a well-understood notion of zero. In all monetary systems, there is a zero and it is equivalent to zero in all other systems. The intervals are fixed. Thus, if you have twice as much in U.S. dollars as I do, it will still be twice as much if we convert both our monies into British pounds (assuming no conversion penalties and using the same exchange rate).

4. Explain why GPA is not sound by measurement theory.

For grade points to be averaged, then grade points must be an interval scale. This implies that the difference between values is comparable. That is, the difference between an A and a B is the same as the difference between a D and an F. Normally, this is not even considered when allocating grades.

5. Why is complexity not readily measurable?

Complexity is not well defined. There are many aspects to complexity, and each person may have a slightly different interpretation of what is complex. In fact, complexity could be considered the interaction between a person and the code.

6. What is the advantage of having a partial order on the empirical relation system?

The empirical relation system must have an accepted relation. It is often easier to find a partial order that is well accepted, whereas finding agreement on all cases might be difficult.

7. Why is the number of decisions plus 1 an important method for calculating McCabe's cyclomatic number?

It would be very time-consuming to have to construct the control flow graph for large programs.

8. Why is monotonicity an important characteristic of a size or effort metric such as Halstead's effort metric?

If adding more code can cause the value of the effort metric to decrease, then the metric's behavior is not understandable. It may also mean that the metric can be manipulated.

Answers to Solved Problems

1. Identify the proper scale for each of the following measures:

LOC	Absolute
McCabe's cyclomatic number	Interval
Average depth of nesting	Ordinal
Maximum depth of nesting	Ordinal

2. Show that the temperature scales of Celsius and Fahrenheit are an interval scale using the Celsius temperatures of 20, 30, and 40 degrees.

The Fahrenheit equivalents are 68, 86, and 104 degrees. The difference between the lowest and middle is 10 Celsius and 18 Fahrenheit. The difference between the bottom and the top is twice that, 20 Celsius and 36 Fahrenheit.

3. Show that McCabe's cyclomatic number satisfies the representational theory of measurement.

For the empirical system, consider the set of all control flow graphs. The relation is that one CFG is less than or equal to the second CFG if the second CFG can be built out of the first by adding nodes and arcs.
   The numerical system (Answer Set) can be the integers. The relation on the integers is the standard less than or equal.
   The mapping is the formula $e - n + 2$. There are only two operations, adding nodes and adding arcs. Adding an arc means increasing the e value. Adding a nodes means adding a node on an arc. This means that both e and n increase by 1, so the value stays the same. Thus, for any two CFGs x and y, if x is less than y, then y can be created from x by adding arcs and nodes. Thus, the value of the mapping must either increase or stay the same. Therefore, the less stringent representation condition is satisfied. (The more stringent representation condition cannot be satisfied, since the order on the CFGs is a partial order).

4. Show that McCabe's cyclomatic number is an interval scale measure.

Since McCabe's cyclomatic number is one more than the number of decisions, every interval in the cyclomatic number is caused by that number of additional decisions. So the difference between 2 and 3 is the same as the difference between 10 and 11. It is not a ratio scale measure because there is not a clear zero. In fact, the cyclomatic number cannot be zero.

5. Calculate McCabe's cyclomatic number on the following source code. Draw a control flow graph. Label the regions with Roman numerals.

```
read x,y,z;
type = ``scalene'';
if (x == y or x == z or y == z) type =``isosceles'';
if (x == y and x == z) type =``equilateral'';
if (x >= y+z or y >= x+z or z >= x+y) type =``not a triangle'';
if (x <= 0 or y <= 0 or| z <= 0) type =``bad inputs'';
print type;
```

See Fig. 5-6 for the control flow graph.

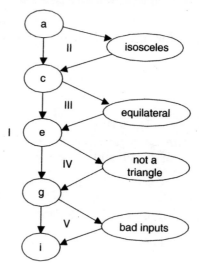

Fig. 5-6.   Control flow graph.

The number of regions is 5, so the cyclomatic number is 5. It can also be counted with decisions. There is a decision about which way to exit nodes a, c, e, and g. Thus, there are 4 decisions. The cyclomatic number is the number of decisions plus 1, so it is 5. It can also be counted using the formula $e - n + 2$. Here, $e = 12$, and $n = 9$, so $e - n + 2 = 5$.

6. Calculate McCabe's cyclomatic number from the control flow graph shown in Fig. 5-5.

Note that the graph is not planar (that is, drawn without crossing lines). Removing arcs until the graph is planar and then counting an additional region for each removed arc can calculate the cyclomatic number. In this graph (see Fig. 5-7), the arc e-g was removed, the regions were counted, and then region VIII was added for arc e-g. The count of decisions is seven (two decisions each on nodes a and c, one decision each on b, e, and f). The $e - n + 2 = 16 - 10 + 2 = 8$.

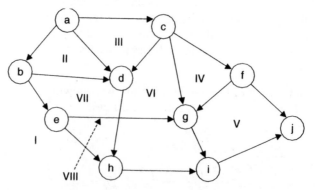

Fig. 5-7.   Control flow graph.

7. Calculate Halstead's basic measures on the triangle code from Problem 5.

operators				operands	
read	1	==	5	string	5
,	2	or	6	x	9
;	7	and	1	y	8
type	6	>=	3	z	8
=	5	<=	3	0	3
if	4	+	3		
( )	4	print	1		

$\eta_1 = 14$ $\eta_2 = 5$ $\eta = 19$ $\eta_2{}^* = 3$
$N_1 = 51$ $N_2 = 33$ $N = 84$
Est N $= 14*\log_2 14 + 5*\log_2 5$
$= 14*3.8 + 5*2.3 = 64.7 + 11.5 = 76.2$
$V = 84*\log_2 19 = 84*4.25 = 357$
$V^* = 5\log_2 5 = 5*2.3 = 11.5$
$L = 11.5 / 357 = 0.032$

8. Calculate Halstead's basic measures on the factorial code given below:

```
int fact (int n) {
      if(n == 0 )
              { return 1 ; }
      else
              { return n * fact (n-1) ; }
      }
```

operators: int 2; ( ) 3; { } 3; if 1; == 1; return 2; ";" 2; else 1; * 1; —1

operands: fact 2; n 4; 0 1; 1 2;
basic counts
$\eta_1 = 10$ $\eta_2 = 4$ $\eta = 14$ $\eta_2{}^* = 1$
$N_1 = 17$ $N_2 = 9$ $N = 26$
Est N $= 10*\log_2 10 + 4*\log_2 4 = 10*3.32 + 4*2.0 = 33.2 + 8.0 = 41.2$
$V = 26*\log_2 14 = 26*3.8 = 98.8$

$V^* = 3\log_2 3 = 3*1.6 = 4.8$
$L = 4.8 / 98.8 = 0.048$

9. Use the code section from the problem statement to draw the control flow graph and calculate McCabe's cyclomatic number using all three approaches. Show which lines of code are represented by which nodes. On the CFG, label the regions with Roman numerals and the decisions with lowercase letters.

See Fig. 5-8.

E = 8, N = 6 (or extra nodes might be at the end of the ifs, so E = 9 and N = 7 or E = 10 and N = 8) => so C = 8 − 6 + 2 = 4
Regions = 4 => C = 4
Decisions = 3 => C = 3 + 1 = 4

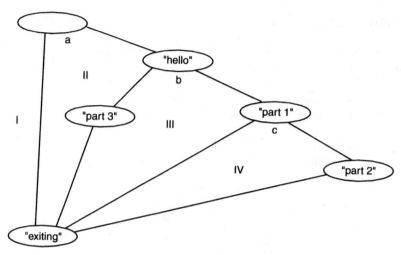

Fig. 5-8.   Control flow graph

10. In Problem 9, count Halstead's η_1 and η_2. Calculate η and N. Count all strings as occurrences of one operand called "string." Show your work.

Operators

token	count	token	count	token	count
cin	1	$\gg$	3	;	6
if	3	( )	3	>	2
{ }	4	cout	5	$\ll$	5
"string"	5	<	1	else	1

Operands

token	count	operands token	count	token	count
a	4	b	2	c	2
10	1				

Note: The quotes could be counted separately from the strings. The else could be counted as part of an if-else so the if would have two occurrences.

$$\eta_1 = 12 \quad \eta_2 = 4 \quad \eta = 16$$
$$N_1 = 30 \quad N_2 = 9 \quad N = 48$$

CHAPTER 6

Risk Analysis and Management

6.1 Introduction

A *risk* is the possibility that an undesirable event (called the *risk event*) could happen. Risks involve both uncertainty (events that are guaranteed to happen are not risks) and loss (events that don't negatively affect the project are not risks). Proactive risk management is the process of trying to minimize the possible bad effects of risk events happening.[1]

There is disagreement about what risks should be managed. Some experts suggest that only risks that are unique to the current project should be considered in risk analysis and management. Their view is that the management of risks common to most projects should be incorporated into the software process.

6.2 Risk Identification

This is the process of identifying possible risks. Risks can be classified as affecting the project plan (project risks), affecting the quality (technical risks), or affecting the viability of the product (business risks). Some experts exclude events that are common to all projects from consideration for risk management. These experts consider those common events as part of standard project planning.

---

[1] Roger Pressman, *Software Engineering: A Practitioner's Approach*, 5th ed, McGraw-Hill, New York, 2001, 145–163.

EXAMPLE 6.1

Consider a project that involves trying to develop safety critical software on cutting-edge hardware. List risks and classify each as project, technical, or business and as common to all projects or special to this project.

Risk	Project	Technical	Business	Common	Special
Hardware not available		X			X
Requirements incomplete	X			X	
Use of specialized methodologies		X			X
Problems achieving required reliability		X			X
Retention of key people	X			X	
Underestimating required effort	X			X	
The single potential customer goes bankrupt			X		X

6.3 Risk Estimation

Risk estimation involves two tasks in rating a risk. The first task is estimating the probability of the occurrence of a risk, called the *risk probability*, and the second task is estimating the cost of the risk event happening, often called the *risk impact*. Estimating the risk probability will be hard. Known risks are much easier to manage, and they become part of the software process. The new risks that are unique to the current project are those most important to manage. The cost of the risk may be easier to determine from previous experience with project failures.

6.4 Risk Exposure

Risk exposure is the expected value of the risk event. This is calculated by multiplying the risk probability by the cost of the risk event.

EXAMPLE 6.2

Consider two dice. Consider a rolling a 7 as an undesirable event that would make you lose a pot of $60. Calculate the risk probability and the risk impact of rolling a 7. Calculate the risk exposure.

The risk probability is 6 cases out of 36 combinations, or 1/6. The risk impact is $60. The risk exposure is 1/6 times $60, or $10.

6.4.1 RISK DECISION TREE

A technique that can be used to visualize the risks of alternatives is to build a risk decision tree. The top-level branch splits based on the alternatives available. The next split is based on the probabilities of events happening. Each leaf node has the risk exposure for that event. The sum of the risk exposures for all leafs under the top-level split gives the total risk exposure for that choice.

EXAMPLE 6.3

A friend offers to play one of two betting games with you. Game A is that you toss a coin twice. He pays you $10 if you get two heads. You pay him $2 for each tail you toss. Game B is that you also toss a coin twice, but it costs you $2 to play and he pays you $10 if you get two heads. Which game should you play?

The risk decision tree is shown in Fig. 6-1. Both games total to $0.50. Thus, each time you play, your average gain is 50 cents. No matter which game you choose.

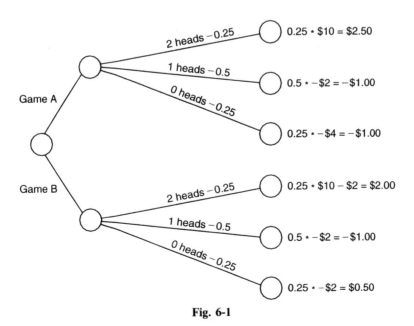

Fig. 6-1

6.5 Risk Mitigation

Risk mitigation is the proactive strategy of trying to find ways to either decrease the probability of the risk event happening or the impact of it happening. While there are no magic ways to reduce risk, a common approach is to try to resolve risks related to uncertainty early. For example, if there is concern about particular systems that need to be used, investigating those systems early is better. Often, a prototype can be built that would identify problems early.

EXAMPLE 6.4

Consider the risks identified in the risk identification problem. Suggest an approach for either decreasing the probability or decreasing the impact or both.

Risk	Decrease Probability	Decrease Impact
Hardware not available	Accelerate dev. of hardware	Build simulator
Requirements incomplete	Increase review of requirements	
Use of specialized methodologies	Increase staff training, hire experts	
Problems achieving required reliability	Design for reliability	
Retention of key people	Pay more	Hire additional personnel
Underestimating required effort	Hire external estimator	Build in slack time, reestimate often
The single potential customer goes bankrupt	Have external evaluation of area	Identify other potential clients

6.6 Risk Management Plans

A risk management plan must include an identifier, a description of the risk, an estimate of risk probability, an estimate of risk impact, a list of mitigation strategies, contingency plans, risk triggers (to determine when contingency plans should be activated), and responsible individuals. Additional fields might include current and/or past status of related metrics.

EXAMPLE 6.5
Develop a form for risk management and insert sample data.

Risk ID: 1-010-77	Prob: 10 percent	Impact: very high
Description: Specialized hardware may not be available.		
Mitigation strategy: Build simulator, accelerate hardware development.		
Risk trigger: Hardware falling 1 week or more behind schedule.		
Contingency plan: Outsource hardware development as backup, deliver system on simulator.		
Status/date/responsible person: Created – Jan 1,01 – Fred Jones Sim. completed – Feb 10, 01 – Bill Olson		

Review Questions

1. Why is risk management important?
2. Consider driving to the airport to catch a plane on an airline that you have not used before. What risks might be unique to this trip to the airport, and which ones might be managed as part of the normal trip to the airport?

Problems

1. Analyze the potential risks for the dental office problem in Chapter 4, Problem 2. Classify the risks as normal or unique to this project.
2. Consider a project that has 0.5 percent probability of an undetected fault that would cost the company $100,000 in fines. Calculate the risk exposure.

3. Consider the use of an additional review for Problem 2 that would cost $100 but eliminate such a fault 50 percent of the time. Calculate this new risk exposure with using the additional review. Is the additional review approach better?

4. What would change in Problem 3 if the additional review was only effective 10 percent of the time?

5. Build a decision tree for the problem in Example 6.3 if in Game A, the payoff was $5.00 and if the cost of playing in Game B was $4.00. Should you play either game?

6. Company X has historical data that shows a normal error rate of 0.0036 errors per KLOC. A study of a new review technique shows that it costs $1000 per 100 KLOC and decreases the number of errors by 50 percent. Assume that each error costs the company an average of $10,000. The current project is estimated to be 50 KLOC in size. Calculate risk exposure for each approach. Is the new review technique worth doing?

 # Answers to Review Questions

1. Why is risk management important?

   Risks can be managed and the effect of risks can be minimized. However, minimizing risk requires that you identify and manage risks.

2. Consider driving to the airport to catch a plane on an airline that you have not used before. What risks might be unique to this trip to the airport, and which ones might be managed as part of the normal trip to the airport?

   Normal risks—Running out of gas, flat tires, weather delays, traffic accidents, forgetting suitcases

   Unique risks—Construction on highway to airport, possibly different terminal, check-in delays specific to this airline

 # Solutions to Problems

1. Analyze the potential risks for the dental office problem in Chapter 4, Problem 2. Classify the risks as normal or unique to this project.

Normal risks—Misunderstanding user desires, miscommunication with user, user hardware problems, cost overrun, project delays, and so on

Unique risks—Interfacing with patient record system

2. Consider a project that has 0.5 percent probability of an undetected fault that would cost the company $100,000 in fines. Calculate the risk exposure.

The risk exposure is the sum of the risk exposure for each possibility.

$$0.005 * 100{,}000 + 0.995 * 0 = \$500$$

3. Consider the use of an additional review for Problem 2 that would cost $100 but eliminate such a fault 50 percent of the time. Calculate this new risk exposure with using the additional review. Is the additional review approach better?

$$0.0025 * 100{,}100 + 0.9975 * 100 = 250.25 + 99.75 = \$350.00$$

The additional review approach is better.

4. What would change in Problem 3 if the additional review was only effective 10 percent of the time?

The risk exposure would increase.

$$0.0045 * 100{,}100 + 0.9955 * 100 = 450.45 + 99.55 = *550.00$$

and be marginally worse than the nonadditional review approach.

5. Build a decision tree for the problem in Example 6.3 if in Game A, the payoff was $5.00 and if the cost of playing in Game B was $4.00. Should you play either game?

The risk decision tree is shown in Fig. 6-2. In both games you would expect to lose money. In game A you would lose an average of $0.75, and in Game B you would lose an average of $1.50.

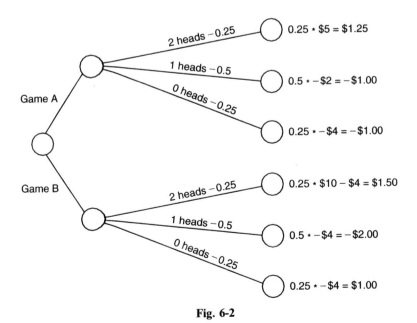

Fig. 6-2

6. Company X has historical data that shows a normal error rate of 0.0036 errors per KLOC. A study of a new review technique shows that it costs $1000 per 100 KLOC and decreases the number of errors by 50 percent. Assume that each error costs the company an average of $10,000. The current project is estimated to be 50 KLOC in size. Calculate risk exposure for each approach. Is the new review technique worth doing?

Case 1—No review

$$0.0036 * 50 \text{ KLOC} * \$10,000 = \$1800$$

Case 2—With review

$$0.0018 * 50 \text{ KLOC} * \$10,000 + \$500 = \$1400$$

Yes, it is better to do the review.

CHAPTER 7

Software Quality Assurance

7.1 Introduction

There are many ways to define quality. None are perfect. It is like the old saying, "I know it when I see it."

One definition is that "quality is the totality of features and characteristics of a product or service which bear on its ability to satisfy a given need" (British Standards Institution).

Another definition is that quality software is software that does what it is supposed to do. The lack of quality is easier to define; it is customer dissatisfaction. The usual measure is defect reports.

The main technique for achieving quality is the software review or walkthrough. The goal of inspections is to find errors. Formal approaches have been shown to work better than informal approaches. The metric used most often to evaluate inspections is errors-found/KLOC. The efficiency may be measured in terms of errors-found/hour-spent. Much experimentation has been done on how much preparation time is optimal. Some work has also been done on how long the inspection meeting should last.

7.2 Formal Inspections and Technical Reviews

A formal inspection is a formal, scheduled activity where a designer presents material about a design and a selected group of peers evaluates the technical aspects of the design.

The details of how a formal inspection or technical review is done can vary widely. The following aspects are usually accepted as what distinguishes a formal inspection from other reviews:

Knowledgeable peers are used.
The producer is an active participant.
An explicit, completed product is inspected.
The primary purpose is to find defects.
A formal inspection is used routinely in software development.
Specific roles are assigned.
The inspection uses the specific steps of formal inspections.
At least three people are involved in the inspection.

7.2.1 INSPECTION ROLES

Although there are variations, the following are the basic roles that most inspections use:

Moderator—The moderator selects the team, conducts the inspection, and reports the results.

Reader—The reader is often not the producer of the product; however, the reader will guide the team through the work product during the inspection meeting.

Recorder—The recorder maintains the records of the inspection and accurately reports each defect.

Producer—The producer is the one who originally produced the product. His or her role is to answer questions during the inspection. The producer is also responsible for correcting any problems identified in the inspection. He or she then reports the corrections to the moderator.

7.2.2 INSPECTION STEPS

Following are the basic steps in an inspection:

1. *Overview*—When the producer satisfies the entrance criteria, the inspection is scheduled. The producer then conducts an overview. It acquaints the rest of the inspection team with the product to be inspected.

2. *Preparation*—The inspection team members study the product. The time spent in preparing is controlled based on the size of the product in KLOC. The members may use a checklist to focus on significant issues.

3. *Inspection meeting*—The moderator supervises the inspection meeting. Some approaches use a reader other than the producer to actually conduct the inspection. The recorder makes a complete record of issues raised. All members of the inspection team sign the report. Any team member may produce a minority report if there is a disagreement.

4. *Rework*—The producer reviews the report and corrects the product.

5. *Follow-up*—The moderator reviews the report and the correction. If it satisfies the exit criteria, the inspection is completed. If not, the moderator can either have the producer rework the product or reinspection can be scheduled.

7.2.3   CHECKLISTS

A checklist is a list of items that should be checked during the review. Sometimes the items are expressed as questions to be answered.

The value of a checklist is that it focuses the attention of the reviewer on potential problems. Every fault that is found should be analyzed to see if it warrants a checklist item to focus on that problem. (I recall a long debugging process caused by a semicolon directly after the condition in an IF statement in C++. Now any checklist for C++ programs I write includes checking for semicolons at the end of decision conditions.)

Checklist items that are not effective in finding faults during inspections should be considered for removal. Too many checklist items will lessen the effectiveness of the inspection.

7.3   Software Reliability

Reliability is the probability of not failing in a specified length of time. This is usually denoted by $R(n)$, where n is the number of time units. If the time unit is days, then $R(1)$ is the probability of not failing in 1 day. The probability of failing in a specified length of time is 1 minus the reliability for that length of time ($F(n) = 1 - R(n)$).

Software reliability is a measure of how often the software encounters a data input or other condition that it does not process correctly to produce the right answer. Software reliability is not concerned with software wearing out. A better analogy for software failures is picking marbles out of a bag or throwing darts blindfolded at balloons on a wall.

7.3.1   ERROR RATES

If an error happens every 2 days, then the instantaneous error rate would be 0.5 errors per day. The error rate is the inverse of the time between errors (inter-error time). The error rate can be used as an estimate of the probability of failure, $F(1)$. Unless we know some trend, the best estimate of the short-term future behavior is the current behavior. So if we find 20 errors on one day, our best estimate for the next day is 20 errors.

EXAMPLE 7.1

If an error happens after 2 days, what is the probability that the system will not fail in 1, 2, 3, and 4 days?

If an error happens every 2 days, we can use 0.5 as the instantaneous error rate. It can also be used to estimate the failure probability for 1 day. Thus, $F(1) = 0.5$. Then, $R(1) = 1 - F(1) = 0.5$. $R(2) = 0.25$. $R(3) = 0.125$. $R(4) = 0.0625$.

If we can see a trend in the error rates, then we can estimate the error rate better. Instead of using equations to fit the data, plots of the failure rate can be used to visualize the behavior.

If x is the inter-failure time, $1/x$ is the instantaneous failure rate. Plot the instantaneous failure rate versus either failure number or the elapsed time of the failure. Try to fit a straight line to the points. The value of the line at the current time can be used for the error rate.

The intersection of this line with the horizontal axis indicates either the fault number where the failure rate goes to zero, or the amount of time necessary to remove all the faults. When the x-axis is the elapsed time, then the area under the straight line (units are time $*$ failure/time) represents the number of faults.

Thus, empirical data about how often the software fails during testing or observation is used to estimate the current rate. Theoretical ideas will be used to refine the predictions for longer periods of time.

7.3.2 PROBABILITY THEORY

$F(1)$ is the probability of failing on the next execution. It is equal to theta, the percentage of test cases that fail.[1] The failure probability can be estimated by the current instantaneous error rate or by the estimated error rate from the error rate plots.

If we know $R(1)$, then the probability that we can execute n test cases without failure is $R(n) = R(1)^n$.

Note that $F(n)$ is not $F(1)^n$. $F(n) = 1 - (1 - F(1))^n$.

7.4 Statistical Quality Assurance

Statistical quality assurance (SQA) is the use of statistics to estimate the quality of software. Executing the code with a small set of randomly chosen test cases will give results that can be used for estimating the quality. This is sometimes called a *software probe*. The error rate on the randomly chosen sample can be used as an estimate of the error rate in the finished project.

If the percentage of correct executions is high, then the development is going well. If the percentage of correct executions is low, then remedial action may be appropriate for the development process.

---

[1] A *failure* is usually defined as external behavior that is different from what is specified in the requirements.

7.5   IEEE Standards for SQA Plan

An important part of achieving quality is to plan for quality, that is, to plan those activities that will help to achieve quality. The IEEE Standards Association has developed a standard (Std 730-1989) for software quality assurance plans.

The following is part of the sections specified in IEEE Std 730-1989:

1. *Purpose*—This section shall list the software covered and the portions of software life cycle covered.

2. *Reference Documents*—This section shall list all the documents referenced in the plan.

3. *Management*

   3.1 *Organization*—This section shall describe the structure of organization and the responsibilities, and usually includes an organizational chart.

   3.2 *Tasks*—This section shall list all of the tasks to be performed, the relationship between tasks and checkpoints, and the sequence of the tasks.

   3.3 *Responsibilities*—This section shall list the responsibilities of each organizational unit.

4. *Documentation*

   4.1 *Purpose*—This section shall list all required documents and state how documents will be evaluated.

   4.2 *Minimum documents*—This section shall describe the minimum required documentation, usually including the following:

   SRS—Software Requirements Specification

   SDD—Software Design Description

   SVVP—Software Verification and Validation Plan

   SVVR—Software Verification and Validation Report

   User documentation—Manual, guide

   SCMP—Software Configuration Management Plan

5. *Standards, Practices, Conventions, and Metrics*

   This section shall identify the S, P, C, and M to be applied and how compliance is to be monitored and assured. The minimal contents should include documentation standards, logic structure standards, coding standards, testing standards, selected SQA product, and process metrics.

6. *Reviews and Audits*—This section shall define what reviews/audits will be done, how they will be accomplished, and what further actions are required.

7. *Tests*—This section shall include all tests that are not included in SVVP.

8. **Problem Reporting**—This section shall define practices and procedures for reporting, tracking, and resolving problems, including organizational responsibilities.

9. **Tools, Techniques, and Methodologies**—This section shall identify the special software tools, techniques, and methodologies and describe their use.

10. **Code Control**—This section shall define the methods and facilities to maintain controlled versions of the software.

11. **Media Control**—This section shall define the methods and facilities to identify, store, and protect the physical media.

12. **Supplier Control** (for outsourcing)—This section shall state provisions for assuring that software provided by suppliers meets standards.

13. **Records**—This section shall identify documentation to be retained and methods to collection, maintain, and safeguard the documentation.

14. **Training**—This section shall identify necessary training activities.

15. **Risk Management**—This section shall specify methods and procedures for risk management.

EXAMPLE 7.2

Develop Section 3 and Section 8 of an SQA plan for a software development project. Assume a project manager named Bill; an external test team consisting of Tina, the leader, Donna, and Helen; a separate configuration management (CM) group consisting of Mike, Sam, and Joe; and a separate external quality assurance (QA) team consisting of John and James.

　　See Fig. 7-1.

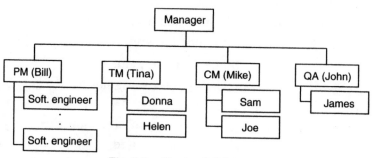

Fig. 7-1.　Section 3 SQA plan.

Section 3

3.1 Organization

3.2 Tasks

All documents will be reviewed. A configuration management tool will manage all documents and source code modules. All test plans will be done during the requirements phase and include an adequate number of test cases. Formal inspections will be conducted at the end of each phase.

3.3 Responsibilities

The project team is responsible for all development, including requirements, design, and implementation. The project team produces the test plan as part of the requirements. They are also responsible for all documentation, including the user manuals and training documents.

The test team is responsible for testing the base-lined version of the source code. The test team will use the test plan developed during requirements. Additional test cases will be developed to satisfy every-statement coverage of the code. Any discrepancies in the test plan and/or requirements or testing will be reported to the overall manager.

The configuration management team will be responsible for accepting software configuration items and assigning version numbers.

The quality assurance team will be responsible for overseeing all reviews, walk-throughs, and inspections. The QA team will track all problem reports.

Section 8

All problems identified outside of the development unit must be reported to the QA team for assignment of a problem report number. The manager of each team will approve the corrections of problem reports assigned to that team. The QA team will be responsible for tracking all problems and weekly reporting to the overall manager.

Review Questions

1. What are the differences between reviews and formal technical reviews?
2. How can you evaluate a checklist?
3. What revisions to a checklist should be done?
4. What factors influence the effectiveness of a formal technical review?
5. How is the effectiveness of a formal technical review measured?
6. What happens if a producer cannot resolve an issue?
7. What happens if one or more members of the inspection team disagree with the majority?
8. If an honest die is rolled 5 times, what is the probability of not seeing a 6 in any of the rolls?
9. If an honest die is rolled 5 times, what is the probability of seeing a 6 on at least one of the rolls?

Problems

1. Build a checklist for reviewing C++ code.

2. Build a checklist for reviewing software designs.

3. Draw a process model for a formal inspection.

4. Assuming that the tests are representative of the operational situation, calculate the reliability of a software system that has had 10 errors in 200 test cases.

5. Assume that FTR technique A requires 2 hours/KLOC preparation and allots 1 hour/KLOC review time and FTR technique B requires 1 hour/KLOC preparation time and 4 hours/KLOC review time. Also assume that in a controlled experiment with the same source code, technique A finds 12 errors/KLOC and B finds 14 errors/KLOC. Compare the two techniques for effectiveness.

6. If the software had 5 failures in 100 tests during 10 days of testing, what would be a good estimate of the reliability of the software over the next day? Week?

7. Develop an SQA plan for the B&B problem (Chapter 4, Problem 3).

8. Error 1 occurred after 4 days, and error 2 occurred 5 days later. Plot the error rate versus error number graph and the error rate versus time graph, and estimate the number of errors in the system and the time to remove all the errors.

Answers to Review Questions

1. What are the differences between reviews and formal technical reviews?

An inspection or formal technical review (FTR) requires an explicit, completed product. The producer must be an active participant in the review/inspection. The inspection/FTR must be part of the defined software process. The primary purpose is to find defects. The inspection must follow the specified process with the specific roles and steps.

2. How can you evaluate a checklist?

Use it in reviewing software code/documents. Record the issues identified with each checklist item. Record the faults found after the item was successfully reviewed.

3. What revisions to a checklist should be done?

Items that are not associated with the detection of faults should be removed. Faults that are detected during later phases of the life cycle should be used to generate new checklist items.

4. What factors influence the effectiveness of a formal technical review?

The preparation time and the review time.

5. How is the effectiveness of a formal technical review measured?

Usually in the rate of discovery of faults. This can be measured both in faults-found/KLOC and in faults-found/reviewer-hour.

6. What happens if a producer cannot resolve an issue?

If the manager cannot resolve the issue, there will probably be a reinspection going through all the phases.

7. What happens if one or more members of the inspection team disagree with the majority?

The minority will produce a minority report presenting their views.

8. If an honest die is rolled 5 times, what is the probability of not seeing a 6 in any of the rolls?

$(5/6)^5 = 0.4018$

9. If an honest die is rolled 5 times, what is the probability of seeing a 6 on at least one of the rolls?

$1 - (5/6)^5 = 1 - 0.4018 = 0.5982$

Answers to Problems

1. Build a checklist for reviewing C++ code.

1. Are all pointers initialized in the constructor?
2. Are all variables declared?
3. Does every "{" have a matching "}"?
4. Does every equality comparison have a double " = "?
5. Are any while or if conditions closed with a ";"?
6. Does every class declaration end with a ";"?

The preceding are sample checklist items I developed based on personal experiences of making C++ faults. In particular, I've spent a long time finding a fault caused by item 5.

2. Build a checklist for reviewing software designs

1. Are all significant functions shown in design?
2. Are all significant attributes specified in design?
3. Are all names related to purpose and type and are they unambiguous?

4. Are all relationships between classes specified?

5. Do all functions have the data necessary for the function to execute?

3. Draw a process model for a formal inspection.

See Fig. 7-2.

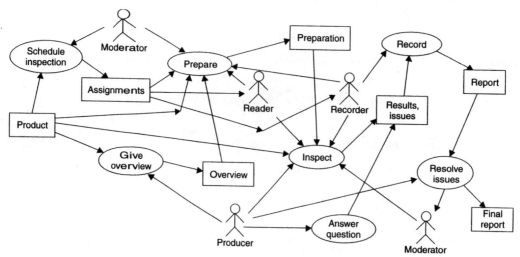

Fig. 7-2.   Process model for inspection.

4. Assuming that the tests are representative of the operational situation, calculate the reliability of a software system that has had 10 errors in 200 test cases.

$F(1) = 10/200 = 0.05$
$R(1) = 0.95$

5. Assume that FTR technique A requires 2 hours/KLOC preparation and allots 1 hour/KLOC review time and FTR technique B requires 1 hour/KLOC preparation time and 4 hours/KLOC review time. Also assume that in a controlled experiment with the same source code, technique A finds 12 errors/KLOC and B finds 14 errors/KLOC. Compare the two techniques for effectiveness.

Technique A took 80 percent of the time of technique B and found 85 percent of the errors that B found. So A is slightly more efficient than B. From the point of view of marginal improvement, it took 2 hours/KLOC more effort to find the last 2 errors/KLOC.

6. If the software had 5 failures in 100 tests during 10 days of testing, what would be a good estimate of the reliability of the software over the next day? Week?

$F(1) = 0.05$ $R(1) = 0.95$

Next day?

Assume 10 tests per day (average from last 10 days). $R(10) = R(1)^{10} = 0.95^{10} = 0.598$.

Next week?

Assume 70 tests. $R(10) = R(1)^{70} = 0.95^{70} = 0.027$.

7. Develop an SQA plan for the B&B problem (Chapter 4, Problem 3).

Section 1. Purpose

The XYZ Corporation is developing software for Tom and Sue's Bed and Breakfast Inn. This software is intended to maintain reservation information and help in monitoring expenses and profits. This SQA plan is for version 1.0 to be delivered to Tom and Sue by November 1.

This SQA plan covers the development life cycle of the complete system from requirements specification through software testing.

Section 2. Reference Documents

Statement of Work, version B&RSOW1.0 dated 1/1
XYZ Corporation Coding Standards, version 4.6, dated 7/8/95

Section 3. Management

3.1 Organization
    Project lead (Tom)
        Development group
            (Bill, Jane, Fred)
        SQA group
            (John)

3.2 Tasks
    Requirements analysis and specification
    Project planning
    Cost estimation
    Architectural design
    Low-level design
    Implementation
    Testing
    Project monitoring
    Inspections
    Reviews
    Documentation

3.3 Responsibilities
    Project Lead—Tom
        Responsibilities: Project planning, cost estimation, project monitoring, approvals of all summary reports and plans
    Requirements Lead—Bill
        Responsibilities: Requirements analysis and specification
        Team members: Jane, Fred
    Design—Jane
        Responsibilities: Architectural design
    Implementation Lead—Jane
        Responsibilities: Low-level design and implementation
        Team members: Fred, Bill
    Test Lead—Bill
        Responsibilities: All testing and test reports
        Team members: Fred
    Documentation—Jane
        Responsibilities: User manual

SQA—John

Responsibilities: Conduct of all reviews, walk-throughs, and inspections, review of all documents and reports, tracking of all problem reports, and submission of weekly problem report

Section 4. Documentation

Software Requirements Specification
Software Design Using UML and OCL
Software Test Plan
Software Test Report
User Manual

Each document will be reviewed in the draft version and inspected in the final version. The SQA lead (John) will be responsible for conducting all reviews and inspections.

Section 5. Standards, Practices, Conventions, and Metrics

XYZ Corporation Coding Standards will be used. The SQA team will conduct inspections of all code to ensure compliance. The compliance report will be submitted to the project lead.

Unadjusted function points will be counted on all components. LOC will be counted on all classes.

Section 6. Reviews and Audits

The following reviews will be done. The SQA lead will conduct each review and submit the report to the project lead for approval.

Reviews:
Software Requirements
Preliminary Design Review
Walk-Throughs of Each Class Design
Code Inspections

Section 7. Test

Testing will be accomplished according to a test plan to be developed by the SQA team and approved by the project lead.

Section 8. Problem Reporting

All problems will be reported to the appropriate lead. If appropriate, the lead will submit a problem report to the SQA lead, who will enter the problem report into the problem tracking system. Resolution of the problem will be reported to the SQA lead. A weekly problem tracking report will be submitted to the project lead.

Section 9. Tools, Techniques and Methodologies

None.

Section 10. Code Control

The XYZ Corporation configuration management system will be used.

Section 11. Media Control

N/A

Section 12. Supplier Control (for outsourcing)

N/A

Section 13. Records—Collection, Maintenance, and Retention

N/A

Section 14. Training

N/A

Section 15. Risk Management

N/A

8. Error 1 occurred after 4 days, and error 2 occurred 5 days later. Plot the error rate versus error number graph and the error rate versus time graph, and estimate the number of errors in the system and the time to remove all the errors.

As shown in Fig. 7-3, plotting error rate versus error number shows an intercept about 6. Thus, there are 4 errors left in the system.

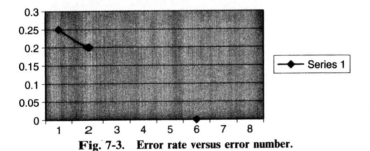

Fig. 7-3.   Error rate versus error number.

As shown in Fig. 7-4, plotting error rates versus time elapsed shows an intercept around 29 to 30. Thus, it should take about 20 more units to completely remove the errors.

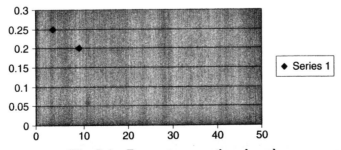

Fig. 7-4.   Error rate versus time elapsed.

CHAPTER 8

Requirements

8.1 Introduction

The goal of the requirements phase is to elicit the requirements from the user. This is usually achieved by the development of diagrams and the requirement specification after discussions with the user. The user then reviews the diagrams and specification to determine if the software developer has understood the requirements. Thus, it is essential that the diagrams and specifications communicate back to the user the essential aspects required of the software to be produced.

The following sections describe the diagrams and requirement specification that are useful in achieving this communication.

8.2 Object Model

The basic approach in an object-oriented (OO) methodology is to develop an object model (see Section 2.4) that describes that subset of the real world that is the problem domain. The purpose is modeling the problem domain and not designing an implementation. Thus, entities that are essential to understanding the problem will be included even if they are not going to be included in the solution. The attributes and methods included in the object model will also be those needed for understanding the problem and not those that will just be important for the solution.

The following are rules for object models for requirements:

1. All real-world entities that are important to understanding the problem domain must be included.

2. All methods and attributes that are important to understanding the problem domain must be included.

3. Objects, attributes, and methods that are only significant for the implementation should not be included.

EXAMPLE 8.1
Draw an object model for the library problem (see Example 2.6).
See Fig. 8-1.

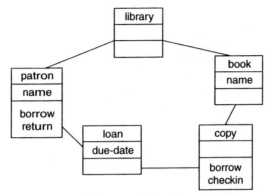

Fig. 8-1.   Object model for library problem.

EXAMPLE 8.2
Draw an object model for simplified vi-like editor.
See Fig. 8-2.

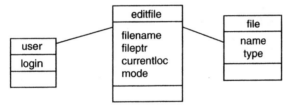

Fig. 8-2.   Object model for simplified vi-like editor.

8.3   Data Flow Modeling

Although not used much in OO development, data flow diagrams (see Section 2.2) were essential parts of pre-OO software development. Data flow diagrams (DFDs) still have an important role in the specification of many systems. The importance of data flow diagrams is in specifying what data is available to a component. Knowing the data available often helps in the understanding of what a component is expected to do and how it will accomplish the task.

EXAMPLE 8.3
Draw a DFD for the simple Unix, vi-like editor.
See Fig. 8-3.

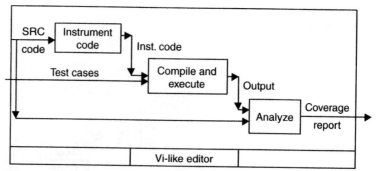

Fig. 8-3.   Data flow diagram for Unix, vi-like editor.

8.4   Behavioral Modeling

Behavioral modeling refers to the behavior of the system, usually from the user point of view. These diagrams are used to specify aspects of the proposed system. It is important that the diagrams capture the essential aspects of the system and are able to communicate those aspects both to the developer and to the user for confirmation that this is the system that he or she wants.

8.4.1   USE CASE

The use case diagram represents the functionality of the system from the user's point of view (see Section 2.5). All critical functionality must be mentioned. However, routine functions that are implied by a higher-level phrase do not have to be specifically mentioned (the danger of miscommunication must be balanced by clarity). The textual requirements will detail these individual functions.

EXAMPLE 8.4
Draw the use case diagram for an editor that is similar to a simplified Unix vi-like editor.
  See Fig. 8-4.

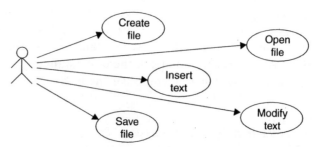

Fig. 8-4.   Use case diagram for editor.

The essential functions in this diagram are file manipulation (create, save, and open). Insert and modify are intended as higher-level phrases covering the typical text-editing functions. Note that some capabilities such as search, copy, and move may be neglected, since they are not mentioned explicitly.

8.4.2   SCENARIOS

A *scenario* is a sequence of actions that accomplishes a user task. Alternative sequences are only shown by having a separate scenario for each alternative. Scenarios are used to illustrate an important capability or proposed use of the system.

In UML, an interaction diagram (see Chapter 2) is used to specify the scenarios. Scenarios can also be specified by listing the sequence of actions.

EXAMPLE 8.5
Write scenarios for the simplified vi editor using each use case in Example 8.4. Use semicolons to separate actions. Use parentheses to contain comments or conditions.

```
Create file
     vi filename (file does not already exist)
Open file
     vi filename (file already exists)
Insert text
     I ; <desired text> ; <esc>
     i ; <desired text> ; <esc>
     O ; <desired text> ; <esc>
     o ; <desired text> ; <esc>
     A ; <desired text> ; <esc>
     a ; <desired text> ; <esc>
Modify text
     cw ; <new text> ; <esc>
     dw
     dd
     x
Save file
     ZZ
```

Note: Not all sequences are shown. For the sake of brevity, not all operations are shown. In an actual specification, efforts should be made to show all operations and significant sequences of operations. In this example, each scenario represents only a part of the use. Alternatively, each scenario could run from open file to close file.

8.4.3   STATE DIAGRAMS

The details of state diagrams were covered in Chapter 2. When being used as part of the requirements specification, it is important that the states reflect domain conditions that are understandable to the users. States that are only significant to the implementation should be coalesced into domain significant states. Additionally, the allowed transitions must include all allowed transitions from the scenarios. Sequences that are not intended in the proposed system should not be allowed in the state diagram. This may be difficult, since the existence of a transition in a scenario does not prohibit other transitions.

The following are rules for using state diagrams in requirement specifications:

1. All states must be domain significant.
2. All sequences from scenarios must be allowed.
3. All prohibited scenarios must not be allowed.

EXAMPLE 8.6
Draw a state diagram for the simple vi-like editor.
    See Fig. 8-5.

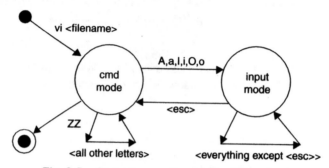

Fig. 8-5. State diagram for simple, vi-like editor.

This state diagram is built by using understanding of the program to coalesce the states into states that have domain relevance. This diagram represents well to the user the behavior of the proposed simple vi-like editor.

8.5   Data Dictionary

A *data dictionary* is a table of information about each data element in the system. Initially, in the requirements phase the data dictionary will be the data items from the problem domain.

A typical entry will include the name of the item, in which class it is located, the type of the data item, and the semantics of the item.

EXAMPLE 8.7
Build a data dictionary for the library problem in Example 2.6.

Name	Class	Type	Size	Semantics
Author	Book	String	< 40 char	Last name, first name (may be truncated)
Book	Book	Object		Abstract concept of the book
Book ID	Copy	Key		Key to info about the book
Borrower	Loan	Key		Key to patron who made this loan
Copy	Copy	Object		Library's physical copy of a book

Copy ID	Copy	Key		Key to physical copy being borrowed
ISBN	Book	String	10-20 char	International Standard Book Number
Loan	Loan	Object		A borrowing that is still active
Name	Patron	String	< 40 char	Last name, first name (may be truncated)
Patron	Patron	Object		Registered holder of library card
Title	Book	String	< 50 char	First 50 char of title from title page

8.6   System Diagrams

A *system diagram* is a nonformally defined diagram used to give an overview of a proposed system. It is often used when the more formally defined diagrams are too limited to express the necessary overview. System diagrams usually incorporate aspects of data flow and use case diagrams. They usually have ovals representing processing parts of the system, data objects representing files and/or databases, boxes representing data, and stick figures representing persons. Arcs are used to show the flow into and out of functions. A challenge with systems diagrams is to maintain consistency in the use of symbols and to give sufficient details.

EXAMPLE 8.8
Draw a system diagram for the simple vi-like editor.
   See Fig. 8-6.

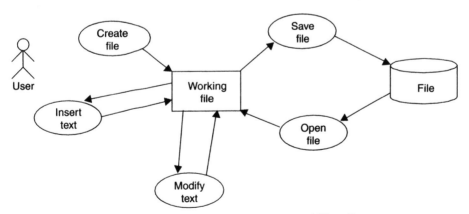

Fig. 8-6.   System diagram for simple, vi-like editor.

EXAMPLE 8.9
Draw a system diagram for a testing tool that instruments a source code, compiles the instrumented code, executes that code with test cases, and then analyzes the results.
   See Fig. 8-7. Note that the output from the compiler process is another process.

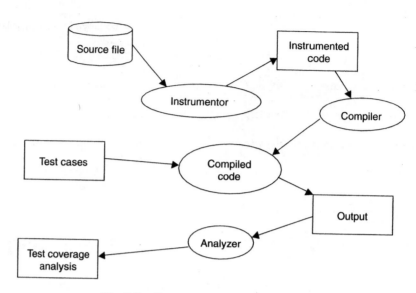

Fig. 8-7. System diagram for testing tool.

8.7 IEEE Standard for Software Requirements Specification

The following SRS outline is based on IEEE 830-1993:

1. *Introduction*—This section is intended to provide an overview of the rest of the specification.

    1.1 *Purpose*—This section must describe the purpose of the SRS and the intended audience.

    1.2 *Scope*—This section must identify the product, explain what the product will and will not do, and describe the application of the software, including benefits, objectives, and goals.

    1.3 *Definitions*—This section must identify all terms, acronyms, and abbreviations used in the specification.

    1.4 *References*—This section must identify all documents referenced elsewhere in the specification.

    1.5 *Overview*—This section must describe what the rest of document contains.

2. *Overall Description*—This section is intended to provide the background to understand the rest of the requirements.

    2.1 *Product Perspective*—This section must put the product into perspective with other products. It will usually include a block diagram of the larger system. It should specify constraints (e.g., system interfaces with other software), user interfaces (e.g., screen formats, timing), hardware interfaces, software interfaces (e.g., versions of interfaced software), memory constraints, operations (e.g., modes of operations), and site adaptation constraints.

2.2 *Product Functions*—This section must include a summary of the major functions of the product.

2.3 *User Characteristics*—This section must include the educational level, experience, and technical expertise of the users.

2.4 *Constraints*—This section must include any other (e.g., regulatory) constraint that is not covered in Section 2.1.

2.5 *Assumptions and Dependencies*—This section must include any assumptions that, if not true, would require changes to the requirements.

2.6 *Apportioning of Requirements*—This section must identify requirements that may be delayed to future versions of the product.

3. ***Specific Requirements***—According to IEEE Standard 830: "This section of the SRS should contain all the software requirements to a level of detail sufficient to enable designers to design a system to satisfy those requirements, and testers to test that the system satisfies those requirements." This is an important criteria to remember: The SRS should be sufficiently detailed so designs and tests can be constructed directly from the SRS. Also, according to IEEE Standard 830: "These requirements should include at a minimum a description of every input (stimulus) into the system, every output (response) from the system and all functions performed by the system in response to an input or in support of an output."

3.1 *External Interface Requirements*—This section must describe all inputs and outputs of the system. This is detailing the information from Section 2.1

3.2 *Functions*—This section must describe all the functions of the system. These must include validity checks on inputs, responses to abnormal situations, effect of parameters, and the relationship of outputs to inputs.

3.3 *Performance Requirements*—This section must describe the static and dynamic requirements.

3.4 *Design Constraints*—This section must describe any constraints on the design.

Review Questions

1. What is the advantage of a DFD over other diagrams?
2. What is the purpose of behavior specifications and diagrams in requirement specifications?
3. What functions are important to include in use case diagrams?

4. What criteria should be used to evaluate scenarios?

5. What criteria should be used to evaluate state diagrams?

6. What is the advantage of a system diagram?

7. What can be a major problem with system diagrams?

Problems

1. Draw an object model for the B&B problem (see Problem 4.3).

2. Draw an object model for the dental office problem (see Problem 4.2).

3. Draw a DFD for the B&B system (see Problem 4.3).

4. Draw a DFD for the dental office system (see Problem 4.2)

5. Draw a use case diagram for the B&B problem (see Problem 4.3).

6. Draw a use case diagram for the dental office problem (see Problem 4.2).

7. Write scenarios for the B&B problem (see Problem 4.3).

8. Write scenarios for the dental office problem (see Problem 4.2).

9. Draw a state diagram for the B&B problem as a whole (see Problem 4.3).

10. Draw a state diagram for the data item reservation in the B&B problem (see Problem 4.3).

11. Draw a state diagram for the dental office problem (see Problem 4.2).

12. Draw a system diagram for the B&B system (see Problem 4.3).

13. Draw a system diagram for the dental office system (see Problem 4.2).

Answers to Review Questions

1. What is the advantage of a DFD over other diagrams?

The data flow through the system and the specific data that is available to each process are clearly shown.

2. What is the purpose of behavior specifications and diagrams in requirement specifications?

The purpose is to communicate an overview of the proposed system to the user to ensure mutual understanding of the overall behavior of the proposed system.

3. What functions are important to include in use case diagrams?

The important functions are those critical functions that convey the required functionality.

4. What criteria should be used to evaluate scenarios?

Every significant sequence of functions needs to be shown from the user's point of view.

5. What criteria should be used to evaluate state diagrams?

State diagrams need to show all possible transitions. Every arc in the diagram needs to have an event that caused the transition. There must also be a path from the start node to every node and from every node to a terminal node.

6. What is the advantage of a system diagram?

Being less formal, it can be more flexible in expressing ideas about the overall system.

7. What can be a major problem with system diagrams?

The lack of formality can lead to ambiguous diagrams with one symbol being used for different ideas.

Answers to Problems

1. Draw an object model for the B&B problem (see Problem 4.3).

See Fig. 8-8.

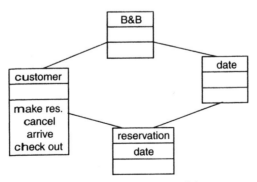

Fig. 8-8. B&B object model.

2. Draw an object model for the dental office problem (see Problem 4.2).

See Fig. 8-9.

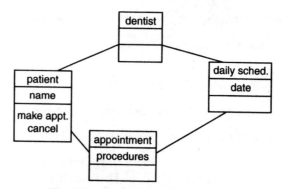

Fig. 8-9.   Dental office object model.

3. Draw a DFD for the B&B system (See Problem 4.3).

See Fig. 8-10.

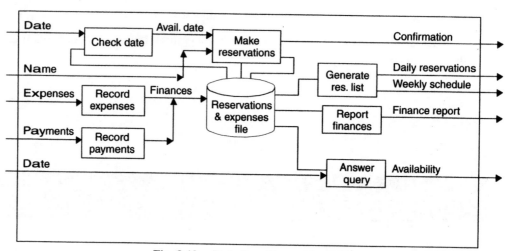

Fig. 8-10.   Data flow diagram for B&B.

4. Draw a DFD for the dental office system (see Problem 4.2).

See Fig. 8-11.

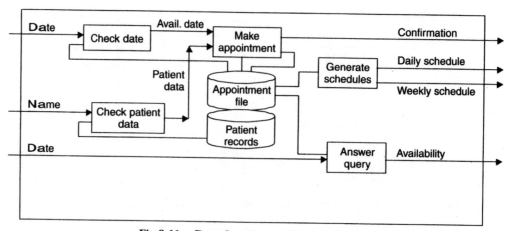

Fig 8-11.   Data flow diagram for dental office.

5. Draw a use case diagram for the B&B problem (see Problem 4.3).

See Fig. 8-12.

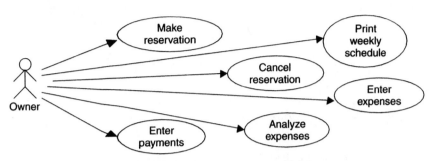

Fig. 8-12.   Use case diagram for B&B.

6. Draw a use case diagram for the dental office problem (see Problem 4.2).

See Fig. 8-13.

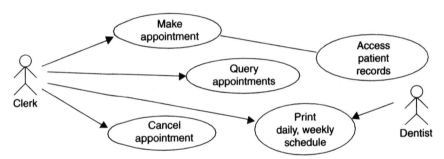

Fig. 8-13.   Use case diagram for dental office.

7. Write scenarios for the B&B problem (see Problem 4.3).

Customer Call 1:

Customer calls about availability on a specified date.
Sue brings up calendar for that week.
There is a vacancy.
Sue quotes a price.
Sue gets name, address, telephone number, and credit card number.
Sue enters information.
Customer provides credit card to guarantee reservation.

Customer Call 2:

Customer calls about availability on a specified date.
Sue brings up calendar for that week.
There are no vacancies.

Customer Call 3:

Customer calls about availability on a specified date.
Sue brings up calendar for that week.
There is a vacancy.
Sue quotes a price.
Sue gets name, address, telephone number, and credit card number.
Sue enters information.
Customer guarantees reservation.
Reserve by date passes.
Another customer requests that date.
Nonguaranteed reservation is removed.

8. Write scenarios for the dental office problem (Problem 4.2).

1—Normal

A patient calls for an appointment. The patient's name is recognized by the system. The system suggests a time. The patient accepts that time, and the receptionist enters the appointment. Two days before the appointment, the receptionist gets a reminder list with the patient's name and phone number. The receptionist calls to remind the patient. The patient comes for the appointment. After the appointment, the dental assistant schedules the patient's next appointment.

2—New Patient

A patient calls for an appointment. The patient's name is not recognized by the system. The patient must be entered into the patient records system.

3—Multiple Appointments

A patient calls and wants to make 6-month appointments for the next 2 years. The receptionist enters his name into the system and, when it is accepted, enters the agreed upon appointments.

9. Draw a state diagram for the B&B problem as a whole (see Problem 4.3).

See Fig. 8-14.

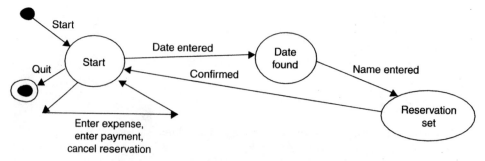

Fig. 8-14.   State diagram for entire B&B problem.

10. Draw a state diagram for the data item reservation in the B&B problem (see Problem 4.3).

See Fig. 8-15.

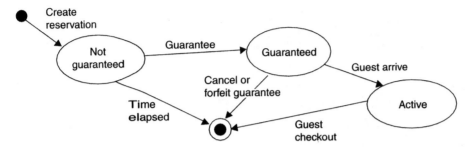

Fig. 8-15. State diagram for data item reservation.

11. Draw a state diagram for the dental office problem (see Problem 4.2).

See Fig. 8-16.

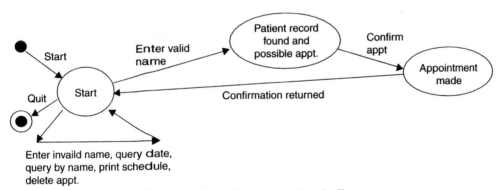

Fig. 8-16. State diagram for dental office.

12. Draw a system diagram for the B&B system (see Problem 4.3).

See Fig. 8-17.

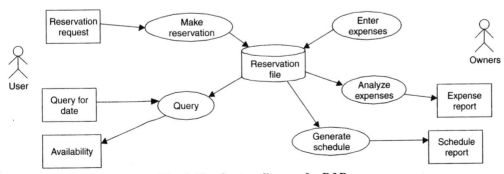

Fig. 8-17. System diagram for B&B.

13. Draw a system diagram for the dental office system (see Problem 4.3).

See Fig. 8-18.

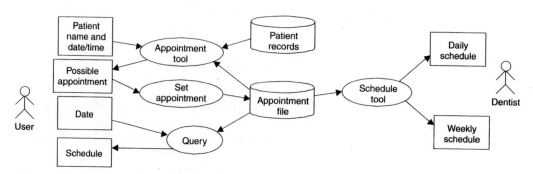

Fig. 8-18.   System diagram for dental office.

CHAPTER 9

Software Design

9.1   Introduction

Design is "the process of applying various techniques and principles for the purpose of defining a device, a process, or a system in sufficient detail to permit its physical realization."[1] Design is also the most artistic or creative part of the software development process. Few rules can be written to guide design.

The design process converts the "what" of the requirements to the "how" of the design. The results of the design phase should be a document that has sufficient detail to allow the system to be implemented without further interaction with either the specifier or the user.

The design process also converts the terminology from the problem space of the requirements to the solution space of the implementation. Some authors talk about object-oriented analysis (OOA) objects, which are in the problem/domain space, and object-oriented design (OOD) objects, which are in the solution/implementation space. For example, in the problem space we can talk about a real-world object like a person; in the solution space we can talk about a C++ class called person.

Gunter et al.[2] write about the phenomenon in the environment (world) and the phenomenon in the implementation (machine). A phenomenon can be visible or hidden. The user-oriented requirements may be expressed in terms of the phenomenon, hidden or visible, from the environment. However, the specification that will be used as the basis for development must sit between the environment and the implementation and must be expressed in terms of a visible phenomenon from each. This specification is the starting point for design and will be called the development specification in this book.

---

[1] Taylor, *An Interim Report of Engineering Design*, MIT, 1959.

[2] Gunter, Gunter, Jackson, and Zave, "A Reference Model for Requirements and Specifications," *IEEE Software*, May/June 2000, 37–43.

EXAMPLE 9.1

A robot is required to find specific brands of pop cans using a black-and-white camera and to return the cans to a recycling location. Such a statement can be the user-oriented requirements and consists of a phenomenon from the environment. However, the pop cans are hidden phenomenon in the environment. That is, the implementation will not know about pop cans; it will know about black-and-white images of pop cans. This is the visible phenomenon. When the specification that will be used as the starting point for design is written, it needs to talk in terms of these images. It will be assumed (and may need to be verified) that only real pop cans will give those images. For example, the problem will be much more difficult if the walls of the environment are covered with ads that contain images of pop cans.

EXAMPLE 9.2

Identify which phenomenon is in the environment and which is in the implementation in the library system.

The physical book is an environment-hidden phenomenon. The system never knows about the book. When the librarian scans the book, he or she is really scanning a bar code. This bar code is not the ISBN but has to reflect possible multiple copies of a single book. This bar code is environment-visible. The implementation probably uses a different identifier or pointer for the book data. This internal identifier is implementation-hidden.

The specification for development needs to be written in terms of the bar code on the book. Neither the physical book nor the internal identifier should be mentioned in the development specification.

9.2 Phases of the Design Process

The following are phases in design:

Data design—This phase produces the data structures.
Architectural design—This phase produces the structural units (classes).
Interface design—This phase specifies the interfaces between the units.
Procedural design—This phase specifies the algorithms of each method.

EXAMPLE 9.3

Design the library classes/data structures from the data items in the object model shown in Fig. 9-1 for the library problem (see Examples 8.1 and 2.6).

The data design and the architectural phases have been combined in this example. The concentration in this example is on the loan and checkout functionality, with little regard for the other necessary tasks, such as administration, cataloging, assigning overdue fines, retiring books, and patron maintenance.

The domain entity "book" is probably not going to continue into the design. It will be combined with "copy" into a class/data structure that stores all the information about a copy. It will probably use the ISBN and a copy number as the unique identifier. The patron information will be stored in a second data structure. Each record is probably identified by an unique patron ID number. The loan information may or may not be a separate data structure. If borrowing information needs to be saved beyond the return of the book, then it had better be a separate class/data

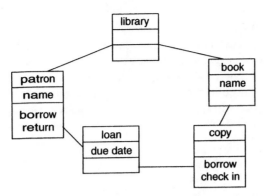

Fig. 9-1. Object model for library.

structure. Otherwise, the patron ID can be part of the copy class/data structure along with the due date of the book.

Note in Fig. 9-2 that many data items have been added that are more in the implementation/solution space than in the problem/domain space. It can be argued that "ISBN" is part of the problem space instead of the solution space, but many library systems do not allow normal users to search by ISBN.

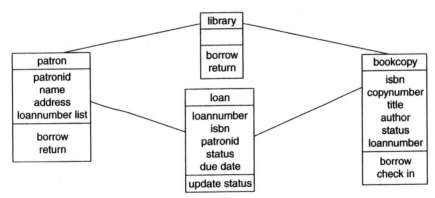

Fig. 9-2. Class diagram for library problem.

9.2.1   INTERFACES

An interface specification is a specification of the external behavior of a module. It should be complete enough so that the calling module knows exactly what the called module will do under any circumstance. It should also be complete enough so that the implementer knows exactly what information must be provided.

The interface specifications in an OO model are often the signatures of the public methods and the semantics associated with the methods. Interfaces can also be specified as part of a formal specification of the behavior of the whole system.

Interfaces can also be the invariants, preconditions, and post-conditions for a method.

EXAMPLE 9.4

Design the interfaces for the `borrow` functions of the library problem using the class diagram produced in Example 9.3.

Both `patron` and `bookcopy` have "borrow" methods. Presumably, calling one or the other of these two methods creates the instance of `loan`. It is not clear from the class diagram which method creates the instance. However, it might be clear if the parameters and return type of each of these methods are specified.

```
method patron::borrow
    input parameters - isbn
    return type - int
        0 if book is not available
        1 if book is available and loan instance created successfully
        -1 if error condition
method bookcopy::borrow
    input parameter - loannumber
    return type - int
        0 if bookcopy is not available
        1 if bookcopy updated successfully
```

9.3   Design Concepts

Two approaches to design are known as refinement and modularity:

Refinement—This design approach develops the design by successively refining levels of detail. Sometimes this is called "top-down" design.

Modularity—This is a structuring approach that divides the software into smaller pieces. All the pieces can be integrated to achieve the problem requirements.

EXAMPLE 9.5

Refine the borrow book function from the library problem.

The top level starts with a function `borrow book` with two parameters, the title of the book and the name of the patron.

The next refinement adds the notion of the `loan` entity. It probably has the following parts: find book given book title, find the patron given patron name, and create loan instance given IDS of book and patron.

The next refinement expands each part. `Find book` returns ISBN if book is found and available, returns zero if book is not found, and returns −1 if book is in use. `Find patron` returns patron ID if patron is found and is in good standing, returns zero if patron not found, and returns −1 if patron is not eligible to borrow books. `Create loan` returns 1 if created successfully.

9.3.1   ATTRIBUTES OF DESIGN

Three design attributes are as follows:

Abstraction—An object is abstract if unnecessary details are removed. Similarly, abstraction in art tries to convey an image with just a few details.

Abstraction in software design tries to let the designer focus on the essential issues without regard to unnecessary low-level details. Good abstraction hides the unnecessary details.

Cohesion—A material is cohesive if it sticks together. A procedure is cohesive if all the statements in the procedure are related to every output. A class is cohesive if all the attributes in the class are used by every method. That is, cohesion in a module is achieved if everything is related. High cohesion is generally considered desirable.

Originally, cohesion was defined in terms of types of cohesion.[3] The types included coincidental, logical, temporal, procedural, communicational, sequential, and functional. Temporal cohesion was when all functions were grouped together, since they had to be performed at the same time. Logical cohesion was when the functions logically belonged together.

Coupling—Coupling is a measure of how interconnected modules are. Two modules are coupled if a change to a variable in one module may require changes in the other module. Usually the lowest coupling is desirable.

EXAMPLE 9.6
Evaluate the abstraction in the borrow functionality in the library problem.

The borrow function appears in three classes: library, patron, and bookcopy. The best abstraction is if the borrow function in library knows as few details about the patron and bookcopy functions as possible. For example, does the borrow function need to know about the loan class?

As shown in Fig. 9-3, if the borrow function in library just calls the borrow function in one of the lower levels, then it has good abstraction. That lower class will be handle the details of creating the loan instance and passing the pointer to the other lower-level class.

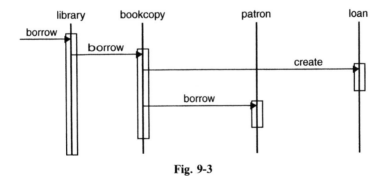

Fig. 9-3

If, however, the borrow function in library knows about the loan class, it can check the availability of the book, create the loan instance, and call both lower-level borrow functions to set the values of the loan instance. (See Fig. 9-4.)

---

[3] W. Stevens, G. Myers, and L. Constantine, "Structured Design," *IBM Systems Journal*, 13 #2, 1974, 115–139.

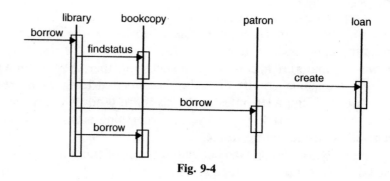

Fig. 9-4

The version in Fig. 9.5 does not have good abstraction. That is, the details of the lower-level classes have not been hidden from the `borrow` function in `library`.

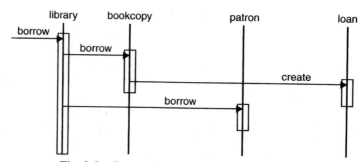

Fig. 9-5.   Borrow interaction diagram—version 1.

9.4   Measuring Cohesion

9.4.1   PROGRAM SLICES

The values of variables in a program depend on the values of other variables. There are two basic dependencies: data dependencies, where the value of x affects the value of y through definition and use pairs, and control dependencies, where the value of x determines whether code that contains definitions of y executes.

EXAMPLE 9.7   MULTIPLICATION BY REPEATED ADDITION
The following code calculates the product of x and y. The output variable z has a data dependency on the variable x, since x is added to z. The output z has a control dependency on the variable y, since y controls how many times x is added to z.

```
z = 0;
while x > 0 do
      z = z + y;
      x = x -1;
end-while
```

Program slices can be calculated from either direction. An output slice finds every statement that affects the value of the specified output. An input slice finds every statement that is affected by the value of the specified input.

It is easier to calculate the program slices from a directed graph that has a set of nodes, n, where each node is an input, an output, or a statement in the code. The arcs, e, are the dependencies.

James Bieman and Linda Ott[4] have used variable definitions and references as the basic units instead of program statements. These definitions and references are called **tokens**. Thus, every constant reference, variable reference, and variable definition is a separate token.

EXAMPLE 9.8

Draw a directed graph showing the dependencies between the variables in the code in Example 9.7. Use solid lines for data dependencies and dashed lines for control dependencies.

From the graph in Fig. 9-6, we can see that the output slice will start from the only output, z. The tokens z, z, y, z, and 0 from the statements $z=z+y$ and $z=0$ are added to the slice. Next, the tokens x and 0 are added from the statement while $x> 0$. Next, the tokens, x, x, and 1 from the statement $x=x+1$ are added. This exhausts the statements, so everything in this program is in the output slice for the variable z.

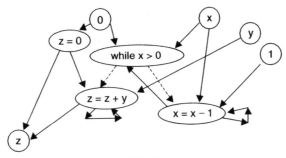

Fig. 9-6

An input slice can start with the input variable x. The tokens x, 0, x, x, and 1 from the statements while $x>0$ and $x=x-1$ are added to the slice. Next, the tokens, z, z, and y from the statement $z=z+y$ are added. No other tokens can be added. Thus, the input slice is everything except $z=0$.

An input slice for the variable y will only contain the initial y token and the tokens z and y from the statement $z=z+y$.

---

[4] James Bieman and Linda Ott, "Measuring Functional Cohesion," *IEEE TOSE*, 20:8 August 1994, 644–657.

9.4.2   GLUE TOKENS

Bieman and Ott also defined some cohesion metrics using output slices. The definitions are based on *glue tokens*, which are tokens (code sections) that are in more than one slice, and *superglue tokens*, which are in all slices. *Adhesiveness of a token* is the percentage of output slices in a procedure that contains the token.

There are three functional cohesion measures:

Weak functional cohesion (WFC)—The ratio of glue tokens to total tokens
Strong functional cohesion (SFC)—The ratio of superglue tokens to total tokens
Adhesiveness (A)—The average adhesiveness of all tokens

EXAMPLE 9.9

Calculate the functional cohesion measures for the following code fragment.

```
cin >> a >> b;
int x,y,z;
x=0; y=1; z=1;
if (a > b){
     x = a*b;
     while (10 > a){
        y=y+z;
        a=a+5;
     }
else {
     x=x+b;
}
```

Fig. 9-7 shows each token from the code. The arcs are drawn from each token to all tokens that are immediately affected by the value of that token.

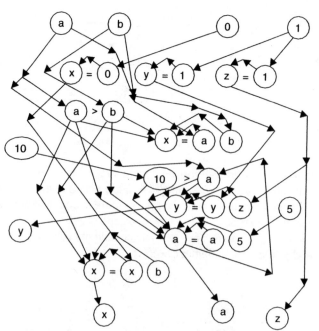

Fig. 9-7.   Directed graph showing all the dependencies.

See Fig. 9-8.

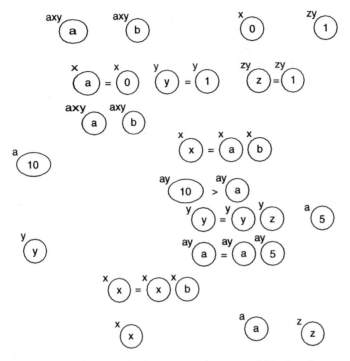

Fig. 9-8. Annotated tokens showing the slices on which the tokens occur.

There are no superglue tokens, so the strong functional cohesion (SFC) is equal to zero. Out of 31 tokens, there are 12 glue tokens, so the weak functional cohesion is 12/31 or 0.387.

There are four slices. Zero tokens have 100 percent adhesiveness. Four tokens are on three slices, so they have 75 percent adhesiveness. Eight tokens are on two slices, so they have 50 percent adhesiveness. The remaining tokens, 19, are on only one slice, so they have 25 percent adhesiveness.

Adhesiveness is the average adhesiveness of all tokens, so

$$(4*0.75 + 8*0.50 + 19*0.25)/31 = 11.25/31 = 0.363.$$

9.5 Measuring Coupling

Coupling is a measure of how closely tied are two or more modules or classes. In particular, a coupling metric should indicate how likely would it be that a change to another module would affect this module. Many coupling metrics have been proposed.

The basic form of a coupling metric is to establish a list of items that cause one module to be tied to the internal workings of another module.

Dharma's Module Coupling

Dharma[5] proposed a metric with the following list of situations to be counted:

di =   Number of input data parameters
ci =   Number of input control parameters
do =   Number of output data parameters
co =   Number of output control parameters
gd =   Number of global variables used as data
gc =   Number of global variables used as control
w =   Number of modules called (fan-out)
r =   Number of modules calling this module (fan-in)

Dharma's module coupling indicator is the inverse of the sum of the preceding items times a proportionality constant:

$$mc = k/(di + 2 * ci + do + 2 * co + gd + 2 * gc + w + r)$$

There are two difficulties with this metric. One is that an inverse means that the greater the number of situations that are counted, the greater the coupling that this module has with other modules and the smaller will be the value of mc. The other issue is that the parameters and calling counts offer potential for problems but do not guarantee that this module is linked to the inner workings of other modules. The use of global variables almost guarantees that this module is tied to the other modules that access the same global variables.

9.6   Requirements Traceability

Requirements traceability tries to link each requirement with a design element that satisfies the requirement. Requirements should influence design. If a requirement does not have a corresponding part of the design or a part of the design does not have a corresponding part in the requirements, there is a potential problem. Of course, some requirements do not have a specific part of the design that reflects the requirement, and some parts of the design may be so general that no part of the requirements requires that section.

One approach to check traceability is to draw a matrix. On one axis will be listed all the requirements items, and on the other will be the list of design items. A mark will be placed at the intersection when a design item handles a requirement.

EXAMPLE 9.10

Draw a matrix showing the tracing of the requirements in the following description of the B&B problem and the design.

Requirements:

---

[5] H. Dharma, "Quantitative Models of Cohesion and Coupling in Software," *Journal of Systems and Software,* 29:4, April 1995.

Tom and Sue are starting a bed-and-breakfast in a small New England town. [1] They will have three bedrooms for guests. [2] They want a system to manage the [2.1] reservations and to monitor [2.2] expenses and profits. When a potential customer calls for a [3] reservation, they will check the [4] calendar, and if there is a [5] vacancy, they will enter [6.1] the customer name, [6.2] address, [6.3] phone number, [6.4] dates, [6.5] agreed upon price, [6.6] credit card number, and [6.7] room number(s). Reservations must be [7] guaranteed by [7.1] 1 day's payment.

Reservations will be held without guarantee for an [7.2] agreed upon time. If not guaranteed by that date, the reservation will be [7.3] dropped.

Design:

```
Class [A] B&B attributes: [A.1] day* daylist[DAYMAX];
    [A.2] reservation* reslist[MAX]; [A.3] transaction*
    translist[TRANSMAX]
    methods: [A.4] display calendar by week
        [A.5] display reservations by customer
        [A.6] display calendar by month
Class [B] day attributes: [B.1] date thisdate
    [B.2] reservation* rooms[NUMBEROFROOMS]
    methods: [B.3] create(), [B.4] addreservation(),
    [B.5] deletereservation()
Class [C] reservation attributes: [C.1]string name
    [C.2] string address [C.3] string creditcardnumber
    [C.4]  date arrival [C.5] date guaranteeby
    [C.6]  int numberofdays [C.7]int roomnumber
    methods: [C.8] create() [C.9] guarantee()
    [C.10] delete()
Class [D] transaction  attributes: [D.1] string name
    [D.2]  date postingdate [D.3] float amount
    [D.4]  string comments
```

	A	A.1	A.2	A.3	A.4	A.5	A.6	B	B.1	B.2	B.3	B.4	B.5	C	C.1	C.2	C.3
1										X							
2	X																
2.1			X							X	X	X	X	X			
2.2				X													
3			X														
4					X	X	X										
5																	
6.1															X		

6.2															X	
6.3																
6.4																
6.5																
6.6																X
6.7																
7																
7.1																
7.2																
7.3																

	C.4	C.5	C.6	C.7	C.8	C.9	C.10	D	D.1	D.2	D.3	D.4
1												
2												
2.1												
2.2								X				
3												
4												
5												
6.1												
6.2												
6.3												
6.4	X		X									
6.5												

6.6											
6.7				X							
7						X					
7.1											
7.2		X									
7.3							X				

As shown in the tables above, there are a number of blank rows and blank columns. Requirement 5 is related to vacancies. There is not explicit handling of vacancies, although a vacancy should be the absence of a reservation on a particular date. Requirement 6.3 is the customer phone number, and it is missing. Requirement 6.5 is the agreed upon price, which is missing from the reservation information. Requirement 7.1 mentions the 1 day's payment, which is also not in the attributes.

Column A.1 is the daylist, which is included to help search for vacancies. B and B.1 are necessary but not specific to a requirement. C.8 is a constructor. D.1 through D.4 are details of the transactions, which are neglected in the requirements.

Review Questions

1. Given the following design, indicate for the following ideas of coupling, cohesion, and abstraction whether it is desirable to have a high or low value and how this design exemplifies the term.

```
Class college
        student* stulist[MAX]
        course* courselist[MAX]
public:
        addStudent(char* studentname)
        addStudentToCourse(char* studentname, char*
        coursename)
        void displayStudent(char* studentname)
        void displayStudentsInCourse(char* coursename)
Class course
        student* classroll[MAX]
public:
        void displayStudents()
```

```
Class student
      char* name
public:
      void displayname()
```

2. Why does Gunter restrict the terms/events that can be used in a specification? What is the difference between a user's requirements and a specification?

3. The proposed system is a face recognition based on image processing. The system will have a camera and is intended to prevent nonemployees from entering the company's secret facilities by controlling the lock on the door. When a person tries to turn the door handle, the system takes an image and compares it with a set of images of current employees.

   Classify each of the following events as to whether the events are in the environment or in the system and whether the events are hidden or visible:

   1.   A person tries to turn the door handles.
   2.   The door is unlocked by the system.
   3.   An employee lets a nonemployee through the door.
   4.   An employee has an identical twin.
   5.   An image has the minimal number of similarities for the matching algorithm.

Problems

1. Draw scenarios for the interaction between a customer trying to buy a particular music CD with cash and a clerk in the music store. Be sure to cover all possibilities. Use the state machine model with the events being the arcs.

2. Calculate Bieman and Ott's functional cohesion metrics for the following code segment. Draw a directed graph and show the flows.

```
cin >> a >> b;
int x,y,z;
x=0; y=1; z=1;
while (a > 0){
    x = x + b;
    z = z * b;
    if (a > b){
          y=y*a;
    }
    a=a-1;
}
cout << x << a << z << y;
}
```

Answers to Review Questions

1. Given the following design, indicate for the following ideas of coupling, cohesion, and abstraction whether it is desirable to have a high or low value and how this design exemplifies the term.

```
Class college
        student* stulist[MAX]
        course* courselist[MAX]
public:
        addStudent(char* studentname)
        addStudentToCourse(char* studentname, char*
        coursename)
        void displayStudent(char* studentname)
        void displayStudentsInCourse(char* coursename)
Class course
        student* classroll[MAX]
public:
        void displayStudents()

Class student
        char* name
public:
        void displayname()
```

   Coupling—Low coupling is desirable, and this design has low coupling, since the college class has no knowledge of the internals of the other classes and the other classes do not need to know about college.

   Cohesion—High cohesion is desirable, and this has high cohesion, since each class just deals with its own attributes.

   Abstraction—The design shows good abstraction. For example, the display method in college does not include any details about lower-level display methods.

2. Why does Gunter restrict the terms/events that can be used in a specification? What is the difference between a user's requirements and a specification?

   Gunter says that a user's requirements must be specified in terms/events that are known to the user and may include terms/events hidden to the machine, while a specification is designed to be the basis of the implementation and must be specified only in terms that are visible both to the machine and the world.

3. The proposed system is a face recognition based on image processing. The system will have a camera and is intended to prevent nonemployees from entering the company's secret facilities by controlling the lock on the door. When a person tries to turn the door handle, the system takes an image and compares it with a set of images of current employees.

   Classify each of the following events as to whether the events are in the environment or in the system and whether the events are hidden or visible:

1. A person tries to turn the door handles. **Environment Visible**
2. The door is unlocked by the system. **System Visible**
3. An employee lets a nonemployee through the door. **Environment Hidden**
4. An employee has an identical twin. **Environment Hidden**
5. An image has the minimal number of similarities for the matching algorithm. **System Hidden**

Answers to Problems

1. Draw scenarios for the interaction between a customer trying to buy a particular music CD with cash and a clerk in the music store. Be sure to cover all possibilities. Use the state machine model with the events being the arcs.

   See Fig. 9-9.

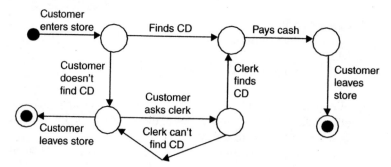

Fig. 9-9. Directed graph.

2. Calculate Bieman and Ott's functional cohesion metrics for the following code segment. Draw a directed graph and show the flows.

```
cin >> a >> b;
int x,y,z;
x=0; y=1; z=1;
while (a > 0){
    x = x + b;
    z = z * b;
    if (a > b){
      y=y*a;
    }
    a=a-1;
}
cout << x << a << z << y;
}
```

See Fig. 9-10.

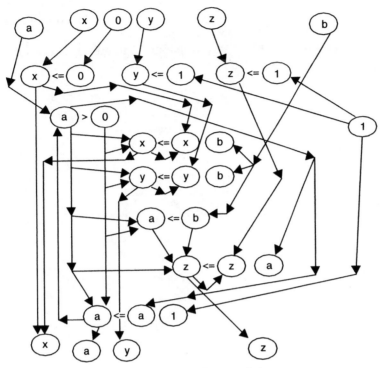

Fig. 9-10. Control flow graph.

See Fig. 9-11.

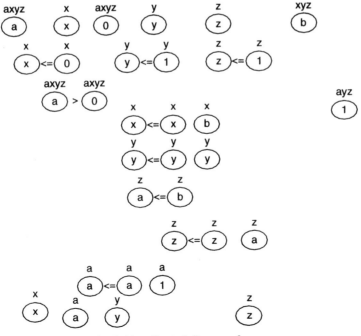

Fig. 9-11. Control flow graph.

There are 33 tokens. Four are superglue. Six (including the superglue tokens) are glue tokens. The weak functional cohesion (WFC) is $6/33 = 18.2$ percent. The strong functional cohesion (SFC) is $4/33 = 12.1$ percent. The adhesiveness is $(4*1 + 2*0.75 + 27*0.25)/33 = 12.25/33 = 37.1$ percent.

This program calculates three separate quantities. It is not surprising that it scores low on the cohesion metrics.

CHAPTER 10

Software Testing

10.1   Introduction

Software testing is the execution of the software with actual test data. Sometimes it is called *dynamic software testing* to distinguish it from *static analysis*, which is sometimes called static testing. Static analysis involves analyzing the source code to identify problems. Although other techniques are very useful in validating software, actual execution of the software with real test data is essential.

10.2   Software Testing Fundamentals

Exhaustive testing is the execution of every possible test case. Rarely can we do exhaustive testing. Even simple systems have too many possible test cases. For example, a program with two integer inputs on a machine with a 32-bit word would have 2^{64} possible test cases (see Review Question 10.1). Thus, testing is always executing a very small percentage of the possible test cases.

Two basic concerns in software testing are (1) what test cases to use (*test case selection*) and (2) how many test cases are necessary (*stopping criterion*). Test case selection can be based on either the specifications (*functional*), the structure of the code (*structural*), the flow of data (*data flow*), or *random* selection of test cases. Test case selection can be viewed as an attempt to space the test cases throughout the input space. Some areas in the domain may be especially error-prone and may need extra attention. The stopping criterion can be based on a *coverage criterion*, such as executing n test cases in each subdomain, or the stopping criterion can be based on a behavior criteria, such as testing until an error rate is less than a threshold x.

A program can be thought of as a mapping from a *domain* space to an answer space or *range*. Given an input, which is a point in the domain space, the program produces an output, which is a point in the range. Similarly, the specification of the program is a map from a domain space to an answer space.

A specification is essential to software testing. Correctness in software is defined as the program mapping being the same as the specification mapping. A good saying to remember is "a program without a specification is always correct." A program without a specification cannot be tested against a specification, and the program does what it does and does not violate its specification.

A *test case* should always include the expected output. It is too easy to look at an output from the computer and think that it is correct. If the expected output is different from the actual output, then the tester and/or user can decide which is correct.

10.3   Test Coverage Criterion

A *test coverage criterion* is a rule about how to select tests and when to stop testing. One basic issue in testing research is how to compare the effectiveness of different test coverage criteria. The standard approach is to use the *subsumes* relationship.

10.3.1   SUBSUMES

A test criterion A *subsumes* test coverage criterion B if any test set that satisfies criterion A also satisfies criterion B. This means that the test coverage criterion A somehow includes the criterion B. For example, if one test coverage criterion required every statement to be executed and another criterion required every statement to be executed and some additional tests, then the second criterion would subsume the first criterion.

Researchers have identified subsumes relationships among most of the conventional criteria. However, although subsumes is a characteristic that is used for comparing test criterian, it does not measure the relative effectiveness of two criteria. This is because most criteria do specify how a set of test cases will be chosen. Picking the minimal set of test cases to satisfy a criterion is not as effective as choosing good test cases until the criterion is met. Thus, a good set of test cases that satisfy a "weaker" criterion may be much better than a poorly chosen set that satisfy a "stronger" criterion.

10.3.2   FUNCTIONAL TESTING

In functional testing, the specification of the software is used to identify subdomains that should be tested. One of the first steps is to generate a test case for every distinct type of output of the program. For example, every error message should be generated. Next, all special cases should have a test case. Tricky situations should be tested. Common mistakes and misconceptions should be tested. The result should be a set of test cases that will thoroughly test the program when it is implemented. This set of test cases may also help clarify to the developer some of the expected behavior of the proposed software.

In his classic book,[1] Glenford Myers poses the following functional testing problem: Develop a good set of test cases for a program that accepts three numbers, *a*, *b*, and *c*, interprets those numbers as the lengths of the sides of a triangle, and outputs the type of the triangle. Myers reports that in his experience most software developers will not respond with a good test set. I have found the same experience in using this example in software engineering classes. Some classes will even fail to include valid triangles in the test set.

EXAMPLE 10.1

For this classic triangle problem, we can divide the domain space into three subdomains, one for each different type of triangle that we will consider: scalene (no sides equal), isosceles (two sides equal), and equilateral (all sides equal). We can also identify two error situations: a subdomain with bad inputs and a subdomain where the sides of those lengths would not form a triangle. Additionally, since the order of the sides is not specified, all combinations should be tried. Finally, each test case needs to specify the value of the output.

Subdomain	*Example Test Case*
Scalene:	
Increasing size	(3,4,5—scalene)
Decreasing size	(5,4,3—scalene)
Largest as second	(4,5,3—scalene)
Isosceles:	
a = b & other side larger	(5,5,8—isosceles)
a = c & other side larger	(5,8,5—isosceles)
b = c & other side larger	(8,5,5—isosceles)
a = b & other side smaller	(8,8,5—isosceles)
a = c & other side smaller	(8,5,8—isosceles)
b = c & other side smaller	(5,8,8—isosceles)
Equilateral:	
All sides equal	(5,5,5—equilateral)
Not a triangle:	
Largest first	(6,4,2—not a triangle)
Largest second	(4,6,2—not a triangle)
Largest third	(1,2,3—not a triangle)
Bad inputs:	
One bad input	(−1,2,4—bad inputs)
Two bad inputs	(3,−2,−5—bad inputs)
Three bad inputs	(0,0,0 – bad inputs)

---

[1] G. Myers, *The Art of Software Testing*, New York: John Wiley, 1979.

This list of subdomains could be increased to distinguish other subdomains that might be considered significant. For example, in scalene subdomains, there are actually six different orderings, but the placement of the largest might be the most significant based on possible mistakes in programming.

Note that one test case in each subdomain is usually considered minimal but acceptable.

10.3.3   TEST MATRICES

A way to formalize this identification of subdomains is to build a matrix using the conditions that we can identify from the specification and then to systematically identify all combinations of these conditions as being true or false.

EXAMPLE 10.2
The conditions in the triangle problem might be (1) $a = b$ or $a = c$ or $b = c$, (2) $a = b$ and $b = c$, (3) $a < b + c$ and $b < a + c$ and $c < a + b$, and (4) $a > 0$ and $b > 0$ and $c > 0$. These four conditions can be put on the rows of a matrix. The columns of the matrix will each be a subdomain. For each subdomain, a T will be placed in each row whose condition is true and an F when the condition is false. All

Conditions	1	2	3	4	5	6	7	8
$a = b$ or $a = c$ or $b = c$	T	T	T	T	T	F	F	F
$a = b$ and $b = c$	T	T	F	F	F	F	F	F
$a =< b + c$ or $b =< a + c$ or $c =< a + b$	T	F	T	T	F	T	T	F
$a => 0$ or $b => 0$ or $c => 0$	T	F	T	F	F	T	F	F
Sample test case	0,0,0	3,3,3	0,4,0	3,8,3	5,8,5	0,5,6	3,4,8	3,4,5
Expected output	Bad inputs	Equilateral	Bad inputs	Not triangle	Isosceles	Bad inputs	Not triangle	Scalene

valid combinations of T and F will be used. If there are three conditions, there may be $2^3 = 8$ subdomains (columns). Additional rows will be used for values of a, b, and c and for the expected output for each subdomain.

10.3.4   STRUCTURAL TESTING

Structural testing is based on the structure of the source code. The simplest structural testing criterion is *every statement coverage*, often called C0 coverage.[2]

10.3.4.1   C0—Every Statement Coverage

This criterion is that every statement of the source code should be executed by some test case. The normal approach to achieving C0 coverage is to select test cases until a coverage tool indicates that all statements in the code have been executed.

EXAMPLE 10.3
The following pseudocode implements the triangle problem. The matrix shows which lines are executed by which test cases. Note that the first three statements (A, B, and C) can be considered parts of the same node.

Node	Source Line	3,4,5	3,5,3	0,1,0	4,4,4
A	`read a,b,c`	*	*	*	*
B	`type=``scalene''`	*	*	*	*
C	`if(a==b||b==c||a==c)`	*	*	*	*
D	`type=``isosceles''`		*	*	*
E	`if(a==b&&b==c)`	*	*	*	*
F	`type=``equilateral''`				*
G	`if(a>=b+c||b>=a+c||c>=a+b)`	*	*	*	*
H	`type=``not a triangle''`			*	
I	`if(a<=0||b<=0||c<=0)`	*	*	*	*
J	`type=``bad inputs''`			*	
K	`print type`	*	*	*	*

---

[2] E. F. Miller developed the C0 and C1 naming system. His work contains many other criteria.

By the fourth test case, every statement has been executed. This set of test cases is not the smallest set that would cover every statement. However, finding the smallest test set would often not find a good test set.

10.3.4.2   C1—Every-Branch Testing

A more thorough test criterion is *every-branch testing*, which is often called C1 test coverage. In this criterion, the goal is to go both ways out of every decision.

EXAMPLE 10.4
If we model the program of Example 10.3 as a control flow graph (see Chapter 2), this coverage criterion requires covering every arc in the control flow diagram. See Fig. 10-1.

Arcs	3,4,5	3,5,3	0,1,0	4,4,4
ABC–D		*	*	*
ABC–E	*			
D–E		*	*	*
E–F				*
E–G	*	*	*	
F–G				*
G–H			*	
G–I	*	*		*
H–I			*	
I–J			*	
I–K	*	*		*
J–K			*	

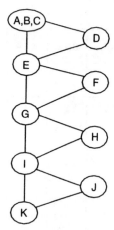

Fig. 10-1.   Control flow graph for Example 10.3.

10.3.4.3   Every-Path Testing

Even more thorough is the *every-path testing* criterion. A path is a unique sequence of program nodes that are executed by a test case. In the testing matrix (Example 10.2) above, there were eight subdomains. Each of these just happens to be a path. In that example, there are sixteen different combinations of T and F. However, eight of those combinations are *infeasible paths*. That is, there is no test case that could have that combination of T and F for the decisions in the program. It can be exceedingly hard to determine if a path is infeasible or if it is just hard to find a test case that executes that path.

Most programs with loops will have an infinite number of paths. In general, every-path testing is not reasonable.

EXAMPLE 10.5
The following table shows the eight feasible paths in the triangle pseudocode from Example 10.3.

Path	T/F	Test Case	Output
ABCEGIK	FFFF	3,4,5	Scalene
ABCEGHIK	FFTF	3,4,8	Not a triangle
ABCEGHIJK	FFTT	0,5,6	Bad inputs
ABCDEGIK	TFFF	5,8,5	Isosceles
ABCDEGHIK	TFTF	3,8,3	Not a triangle
ABCDEGHIJK	TFTT	0,4,0	Bad inputs
ABCDEFGIK	TTFF	3,3,3	Equilateral
ABCDEFGHIJK	TTTT	0,0,0	Bad inputs

10.3.4.4   Multiple-Condition Coverage

A multiple-condition testing criterion requires that each primitive relation condition is evaluated both true and false. Additionally, all combinations of T/F for the primitive relations in a condition must be tried. Note that lazy evaluation[3] of expressions will eliminate some combinations. For example, in an "and" of two primitive relations, the second will not be evaluated if the first one is false.

EXAMPLE 10.6
In the pseudocode in Example 10.3, there are multiple conditions in each decision statement. Primitives that are not executed because of lazy evaluation are shown with an "X".

---

[3] A compiler does lazy evaluation when it does not generate code for tests that are not needed. For example, if the first condition of an "or" expression is true, the second condition does not need to be tested.

`if(a==b||b==c||a==c)`

Combination	Possible Test Case	Branch
TXX	3,3,4	ABC-D
FTX	4,3,3	ABC-D
FFT	3,4,3	ABC-D
FFF	3,4,5	ABC-E

`if(a==b&&b==c)`

Combination	Possible Test Case	Branch
TT	3,3,3	E-F
TF	3,3,4	E-G
FX	4,3,3	E-G

`if(a>=b+c||b>=a+c||c>=a+b)`

Combination	Possible Test Case	Branch
TXX	8,4,3	G-H
FTX	4,8,3	G-H
FFT	4,3,8	G-H
FFF	3,3,3	G-I

`if(a<=0||b<=0||c<=0)`

Combination	Possible Test Case	Branch
TXX	0,4,5	I-J
FTX	4,-2,-2	I-J
FFT	5,4,-3	I-J
FFF	3,3,3	I-K

10.3.4.5   Subdomain Testing

Subdomain testing is the idea of partitioning the input domain into mutually exclusive subdomains and requiring an equal number of test cases from each subdomain. This was basically the idea behind the test matrix. Subdomain testing is more general in that it does not restrict how the subdomains are selected. Generally, if there is a good reason for picking the subdomains, then they may be useful for testing. Additionally, the subdomains from other approaches might be subdivided into smaller subdomains. Theoretical work has shown that subdividing subdomains is only effective if it tends to isolate potential errors into individual subdomains.

Every-statement coverage and every-branch coverage are not subdomain tests. There are not mutually exclusive subdomains related to the execution of different statements or branches. Every-path coverage is a subdomain coverage, since the subdomain of test cases that execute a particular path through a program is mutually exclusive with the subdomain for any other path.

EXAMPLE 10.7

For the triangle problem, we might start with a subdomain for each output. These might be further subdivided into new subdomains based on whether the largest or the bad element is in the first position, second position, or third position (when appropriate).

Subdomain	Possible Test Case
Equilateral	3,3,3
Isos – first	8,5,5
Isos – sec	5,8,5
Isos – third	5,5,8
Scalene – first	5,4,3
Scalene – sec	4,5,3
Scalene – third	3,4,5

Subdomain	Possible Test Case
Not triangle – first	8,3,3
Not triangle – sec	3,8,4
Not triangle – third	4,3,8
Bad input – first	0,3,4
Bad input – sec	3,0,4
Bad input – third	3,4,0

10.3.4.6 C1 Subsumes C0

EXAMPLE 10.8—C1 Subsumes C0
For the triangle problem, in Example 10.3 we selected good test cases until we achieved the C0 coverage. The test cases were (3,4,5—scalene), (3,5,3—isosceles), (0,1,0—bad inputs), and (4,4,4—equilateral). These tests also covered four out the five possible outputs. However, we can achieve C1 coverage with two test cases: (3,4,5—scalene) and (0,0,0—bad inputs). This test is probably not as good as the first test set. However, it achieves C1 coverage and it also achieves C0 coverage.

10.4   Data Flow Testing

Data flow testing is testing based on the flow of data through a program. Data flows from where it is defined to where it is used. A *definition of data*, or *def*, is when a value is assigned to a variable. Two different kinds of use have been identified. The *computation use*, or *c-use*, is when the variable appears on the right-hand side of an assignment statement. A c-use is said to occur on the assignment statement. The *predicate use*, or *p-use*, is when the variable is used in the condition of a decision statement. A p-use is assigned to both branches out of the decision statement. A *definition free path*, or *def-free*, is a path from a definition of a variable to a use of that variable that does not include another definition of the variable.

EXAMPLE 10.9—Control Flow Graph of Triangle Problem (Example 10.3)
The control flow graph in Fig. 10-2 is annotated with the definitions and uses of the variables *a,b,* and *c.*

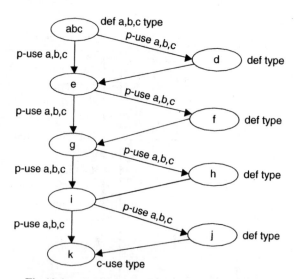

Fig 10-2.   Control flow graph of triangle problem.

There are many data flow testing criteria. The basic criteria include *dcu*, which requires a def-free path from every definition to a c-use; *dpu*, which requires a def-free path from every definition to a p-use; and *du*, which requires a def-free path from every definition to every possible use. The most extensive criteria is *all-du-paths*, which requires all def-free paths from every definition to every possible use.

EXAMPLE 10.10—Data Flow Testing of Triangle Problem

dcu—The only c-use is for variable type in node k (the output statement).

From def type in node abc to node k	Path abc,e,g,i,k
From def type in node d to node k	Path d,e,g,i,k
From def type in node f to node k	Path f,g,i,k
From def type in node h to node k	Path h,i,k
From def type in node j to node k	Path j,k

dpu—The only p-use is for variables a,b,c and the only def of a,b,c is node abc.

From node abc to arc abc-d
From node abc to arc abc-e
From node abc to arc e-f
From node abc to arc e-g
From node abc to arc g-h
From node abc to arc g-i
From node abc to arc i-j
From node abc to arc i-k

du—All defs to all uses.
  All test cases of dcu and dpu combined.

all-du-paths—All def-free paths from all defs to all uses.
  Same as du tests.

10.5   Random Testing

Random testing is accomplished by randomly selecting the test cases. This approach has the advantage of being fast and it also eliminates biases of the testers. Additionally, statistical inference is easier when the tests are selected randomly. Often the tests are selected randomly from an operational profile.

EXAMPLE 10.11

For the triangle problem, we could use a random number generator and group each successive set of three numbers as a test set. We would have the additional work of determining the expected output. One problem with this is that the chance of ever generating an equilateral test case would be very small. If it actually happened, we would probably start questioning our pseudorandom number generator.

10.5.1 OPERATIONAL PROFILE

Testing in the development environment is often very different than execution in the operational environment. One way to make these two more similar is to have a specification of the types and the probabilities that those types will be encountered in the normal operations. This specification is called an *operational profile*. By drawing the test cases from the operational profile, the tester will have more confidence that the behavior of the program during testing is more predictive of how it will behave during operation.

EXAMPLE 10.12

A possible operational profile for the triangle problem is as follows:

#	Description	Probability
1	equilateral	.20
2	isosceles – obtuse	.10
3	isosceles – right	.20
4	scalene – right triangle	.10
5	scalene – all acute	.25
6	scalene – obtuse angle	.15

To apply random testing, the tester might generate a number to select the category by probabilities and then sufficient additional numbers to create the test case. If the category selected was the equilateral case, the tester would use the same number for all three inputs. An isosceles–right would require a random number for the length of the two sides, and then the use of trigonometry to calculate the other side.

10.5.2 STATISTICAL INFERENCE FROM TESTING

If random testing has been done by randomly selecting test cases from an operational profile, then the behavior of the software during testing should be the same as its behavior in the operational environment.

EXAMPLE 10.13
If we selected 1000 test cases randomly using an operational profile and found three errors, we could predict that this software would have an error rate of less than three failures per 1000 executions in the operational environment. See Section 3.8 for more information on using error rates.

10.6 Boundary Testing

Often errors happen at boundaries between domains. In source code, decision statements determine the boundaries. If a decision statement is written as x<1 instead of x<0, the boundary has shifted. If a decision is written x=<1, then the boundary, x=1, is in the true subdomain. In the terminology of boundary testing, we say that the **on tests** are in the true domain and the **off tests** are values of x greater than 1 and are in the false domain.

If a decision is written $x < 1$ instead of $x = < 1$, then the boundary, $x = 1$, is now in the false subdomain instead of in the true subdomain.

Boundary testing is aimed at ensuring that the actual boundary between two subdomains is as close as possible to the specified boundary. Thus, test cases are selected on the boundary and off the boundary as close as reasonable to the boundary. The standard boundary test is to do two on tests as far apart as possible and one off test close to the middle of the boundary.

Figure 10-3 shows a simple boundary. The arrow indicates that the on tests of the boundary are in the subdomain below the boundary. The two on tests are at the ends of the boundary and the off test is just above the boundary halfway along the boundary.

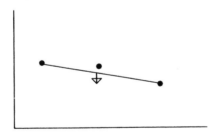

Fig. 10-3.   Boundary conditions.

EXAMPLE 10.14
In the triangle example, the primitive conditions, $a => b + c$ or $b => a + c$ or $c => a + b$, determine a boundary. Since these are in three variables, the boundary is actually a plane in 3D space. The on tests would be two (or more) widely separated tests that have equality—for example, (8,1,7) and (8,7,1). These are both true. The off test would be in the other domain (false) and would be near the middle—for example, (7.9, 4,4).

Note: For a discussion of object-oriented (OO) testing, see Chapter 13.

Review Questions

1. What are the basic concerns with software testing?
2. Why is a specification needed in order to do testing?
3. Why is path testing usually impractical?
4. Does path testing subsume statement coverage?
5. Software testers have sometimes said "errors happen in corners." What could this mean?
6. Every-statement coverage is not a subdomain testing criterion. What is the significance of this?
7. How would the operational profile be different for a point-of-sale terminal in a discount store from a point-of-sale terminal in a ritzy store?
8. A software developer may unconsciously not test his or her software thoroughly. Why would a testing coverage criterion help?

Problems

1. If a program has two integer inputs and each can be 32-bit integer, how many possible inputs does this program have?
2. If a program has 2^{64} possible inputs and one test can be run every millisecond, how long would it take to execute all of the possible inputs?
3. A payroll program will calculate the weekly gross pay given an input of the number of hours worked and current wages. A worker may not work more than 80 hours per week, and the maximum wage is $50.00 per hour. Construct functional tests.
4. A program calculates the area of a triangle. The inputs are three sets of x,y coordinates. Construct functional tests.
5. A program accepts two times (in 12-hour format) and outputs the elapsed number of minutes. Construct functional tests.
6. A binary search routine searches a list of names in alphabetical order and returns true if the name is in the list and returns false otherwise. Construct functional tests.
7. For the payroll program in Problem 10.3, identify the conditions and construct the test matrix.
8. For the area of the triangle calculation of Problem 10.4, identify the conditions and construct the test matrix.
9. For the elapsed time calculator of Problem 10.5, identify the conditions and construct the test matrix.

10. For the binary search routine of Problem 10.6, identify the conditions and construct the test matrix.

11. Find the minimal set of test cases that would achieve C0 and C1 coverage of the triangle problem pseudocode from Example 10.3.

12. The following pseudocode implements the elapsed time problem of Problem 10.5 if the elapsed time is less than 24 hours. Select test cases until every-statement coverage is achieved. Select additional test cases to achieve every-branch coverage.

```
read hr1 min1 AmOrPm1
read hr2 min2 AmOrPm2
if (hr1 == 12)
      hr1 = 0
if (hr2 == 12)
      hr2 = 0
if (AmOrPm1 == pm)
      hr1 = hr1 + 12
if (AmOrPm2 == pm)
      hr2 = hr2 + 12
if ( min2 < min1)
      min2 = min2 + 1
      hr2 = hr2 - 1
if( hr2 < hr1)
      hr2 = hr2 + 24
elapsed = min2 - min1 + 60* (hr2 - hr1)
print elapsed
```

13. For the pseudocode of Problem 10.12, find a minimal set of test cases that will achieve C0 and a minimal set of test cases that will achieve C1.

14. For the following code, identify all feasible paths, path tests, and data flow tests:

```
cin >> a >> b >> c; // node A
x = 5; y = 7;
if ( a > b && b > c) {
      a = a + 1; // node B
      x = x + 6;
      if ( a = 10 || b > 20) {
            b = b + 1; // node C
            x = y + 4;
            }
      if (a < 10 || c = 20) { // node D
            b = b + 2; // node E
            y = 4
            }
      a = a + b + 1; // node F
      y = x + y;
      }
if (a > 5 || c < 10) { // node G
      b = c + 5; // node H
      x = x + 1;
      }
cout >> x >> y; // node I
```

15. Given the following code, draw the CFG and generate a minimal set of test cases for each of the following criteria: C0, C1, dpu, and dcu.

```
cin>> a >> b // node A
if (b>a) {
        x = b; // node B
        if (b>20) {
                x = x + 9; // node C
        }
        else {
                x = x + 1; // node D
        }
        x = x + 1; // node E
}
else {
        x = a // node F
        if (a > 20_ {
                x = x + 15; // node G
        }
        x = x - 5; // node H
}
if (b > a + 20) // node I
{
        x = 20; // node J
}
cout << x; // node K
```

Answers to Review Questions

1. What are the basic concerns with software testing?

The basic concerns are how to select test cases and when to stop testing.

2. Why is a specification needed in order to do testing?

A specification is needed to decide when the actual behavior is correct or incorrect.

3. Why is path testing usually impractical?

Most programs have an infinite number of possible paths through the program.

4. Does path testing subsume statement coverage?

Yes, every statement is on some path. So covering every path will cover every statement.

5. Software testers have sometimes said "errors happen in corners." What could this mean?

Errors tend to be more prevalent on boundaries. That is, faults in the source code often affect some decision and thus produce an error on the boundary.

6. Every statement coverage is not a subdomain testing criterion. What is the significance of this?

When using a subdomain testing criterion, it is easy to improve the coverage by picking multiple test cases from every subdomain. This is also easy to analyze. This is not the case with every-statement coverage.

7. How would the operational profile be different for a point-of-sale terminal in a discount store from a point-of-sale terminal in an expensive store?

In the discount store, there will be more items marked with prices less than $10. In an expensive store, there will be more large prices. The prices may also be rounded up to the next amount.

8. A software developer may unconsciously not test his or her software thoroughly. Why would testing a coverage criterion help?

A testing coverage criterion helps to force the tester to test many different parts of the software.

Answers to Problems

1. If a program has two integer inputs and each can be 32-bit integer, how many possible inputs does this program have?

Each 32-bit integer has 2^{32} possible values. Thus, a program with two integer inputs would have 2^{64} possible inputs.

2. If a program has 2^{64} possible inputs and one test can be run every millisecond, how long would it take to execute all of the possible inputs?

That would be 10^6 tests per second, or $8.64 * 10^{10}$ tests per day. That is equivalent to $3.139 * 10^{13}$ tests per year. Since $2^{10} = 1024$ is about equal to $1000 = 10^3$, $2^{64} = (2^{10})^{6.4}$ and is about equal to $(10^3)^{6.4} = 10^{19.2}$. Dividing $10^{19.2}$ by 10^{13} give a value more than 10^5. Thus it would take at least 10^5 years to do all those tests.

3. A payroll program will calculate the weekly gross pay given an input of the number of hours worked and current wages. A worker may not work more than 80 hours per week, and the maximum wage is $50.00 per hour. Construct functional tests.

Functional tests should include tests of normal pay and overtime and tests of the error conditions.

Hours	Wages	Expected Output
30	40.00	1200.00
60	50.00	3500.00 (assume overtime)
81	50.00	Invalid hours
20	60.00	Invalid wages

4. A program calculates the area of a triangle. The inputs are three sets of x,y coordinates. Construct functional tests.

The functional tests should include correct triangles, non-triangles, error conditions, and the obvious orientation of the triangles.

Point 1	Point 2	Point 3	Expected Area
1,1	1,5	5,1	8
1,1	1,5	1,10	Not a triangle
10,10	0,10	10,0	50
0,0	0,10	10,10	50
0,0	0,0	0,0	0

5. A program accepts two times (in 12-hour format) and outputs the elapsed number of minutes. Construct functional tests.

The functional tests should include tests of less than 1 hour, more than 1 hour, one more than 12 hours, one that requires a carry of hours, and one with the times reversed.

Start Time	Stop Time	Expected Elapsed Time
10:00 a.m.	10:40 a.m.	0:40
9:57 p.m.	11:40 p.m.	1:43
3:00 a.m.	9:15 p.m.	18:15
1:50 a.m.	3:40 a.m.	1:50
3:00 a.m.	7:24 a.m.	4:24
5:00 p.m.	4:00 a.m.	Error

6. A binary search routine searches a list of names in alphabetical order and returns true if the name is in the list and returns false otherwise. Construct functional tests.

The functional tests should include tests of the following:

The first name in the list
The last name in the list
A name before the first name
A name after the last name
A name in the middle
A name not in the list right after the first name
A name not in the list right before the last name

7. For the payroll program in Problem 10.3, identify the conditions and construct the test matrix.

Condition						
0 < hours < = 40	T	F	F	F	T	F
40 < hours < = 80	F	T	F	T	F	F
0 < wages < = 50	T	T	T	F	F	F
Hours	30	50	90	50	30	−5
Wages	50	30	30	60	70	−5
Expected output	1500	1650	Error	Error	Error	Error

8. For the area of the triangle calculation of Problem 10.4, identify the conditions and construct the test matrix.

Conditions		
Collinear pts	F	T
Point 1	10,0	0,0
Point 2	10,10	0,5
Point 2	0,10	0,10
Expected area	50	Error

9. For the elapsed time calculator of Problem 10.5, identify the conditions and construct the test matrix.

There are no conditions specified on the time. The only conditions could be that the times are valid times.

10. For the binary search routine of Problem 10.6, identify the conditions and construct the test matrix.

There are no conditions specified on the search.

11. Find the minimal set of test cases that would achieve C0 and C1 coverage of the triangle problem pseudocode from Example 10.3.

C0 can be achieved with one test case of three equal values less than or equal to zero, e.g., 0,0,0.
C1 can be achieved with two test cases: 0,0,0 and a scalene, e.g., 3,4,5.

12. The following pseudocode implements the elapsed time problem of Problem 10.5 if the elapsed time is less than 24 hours. Select test cases until every-statement coverage is achieved. Select additional test cases to achieve every-branch coverage

```
read hr1 min1 AmOrPm1
read hr2 min2 AmOrPm2
if (hr1 == 12)
        hr1 = 0
if (hr2 == 12)
        hr2 = 0
if (AmOrPm1 == pm)
        hr1 = hr1 + 12
if (AmOrPm2 == pm)
        hr2 = hr2 + 12
```

```
if ( min2 < min1)
      min2 = min2 + 1
      hr2 = hr2 - 1
if( hr2 < hr1)
      hr2 = hr2 + 24
elapsed = min2 - min1 + 60* (hr2 - hr1)
print elapsed
```

C0—Start Time	Stop Time	Expected Elapsed Time
12:00 p.m.	12:40 p.m.	0:40
9:57 p.m.	11:40 p.m.	1:43
5:00 p.m.	4:00 a.m.	12:00

C1—Start Time	Stop Time	Expected Elapsed Time
Tests above plus the following:		
8:00 a.m.	12:40 p.m.	4:40

13. For the pseudocode of Problem 10.12, find a minimal set of test cases that will achieve C0 and a minimal set of test cases that will achieve C1.

The minimal test set for C0 will need at least two test cases. Hour 1 has to be 12 on one test, hour 2 has to be 12 on one test, hour 1 has to be p.m. on one test, hour 2 has to be p.m. on one test, minute 2 has to be less than minute 1 on one test and hour 2 has to be less than hour 1 on one test. This can be done on two test cases.

Min C0—Start Time	Stop Time	Expected Elapsed Time
12:00 p.m.	10:40 a.m.	22:40
9:57 a.m.	12:40 p.m.	2:43

This also achieves C1 coverage because each of those conditions is also false on one of these tests.

14. The following are the feasible paths, path tests, and data flow tests.

Paths	Truth	a,b,c
AGI	FxxF	4,8,12
AGHI	FxxT	4,8,8
ABDFGI	TFFF	Infeasible
ABDFGHI	TFFT	12,8,6
ABCDGI	TTFF	Infeasible
ABCDGHI	TTFT	24,22,8
ABCDEFGI	TTTF	Infeasible
ABCDEFGHI	TTTT	24,22,20
ABDEFGI	TFTF	Infeasible
ABDEFGHI	TFTT	6,4,2

Node	def	c-use	p-use
A	a,b,c,x,y		
ab,ag			a,b,c
B	a,x	a,x	
bc,bd			a,b
C	b,x	b,y	
D			
de,df			a,c
E	b,y	b	
F	a,y	a,b,x,y	

G			
gh,gi			a,c
H	b,x	c,x	
I		x,y	

See Fig. 10-4.

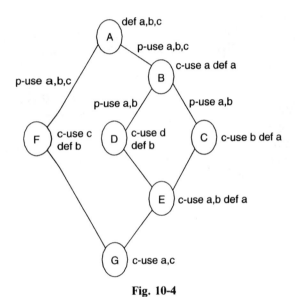

Fig. 10-4

15. The following are the paths, CFG, and minimal test cases for each of the following criteria: C0, C1, dpu, and dcu.

Paths (feasible are numbered)

1. abceik   TTF
2. abceijk   TTT
3. abdeik   TFF
4 .abdeijk   TTT
5. afhik   FTF
afhijk   infeasible
6. afghik   FFF
afghijk   infeasible

Minimal tests:

C0:   inputs   output
2. abceijk   10,30   20
3. abdeik   10,20   22
6. afghik   20,15   30
(must include 6, but could be 1 and 4)

C1:   inputs   output
C0 tests plus
6. afghik   20,15   30
(must include 6, but could be paths 1 and 4)

dpu: The only p-uses are for variable a and b. The only defs for a and b are in node
       A. The minimal test set is equivalent to C1. It must include partial paths AB,
       AF, BC, BD, FH, FG, IJ, and IK. This can be done with paths 1,4,5,6 or
       paths 2,3,5,6

dcu: The defs of variable x are in nodes B,C,D,E,F,G,H, and J. The c-use for
       variable x are in nodes C,D,E,G,H, and K. The defs of variables a and b
       are in node A and the c-use of variable b is in node B and the c-use of variable
       a is in node F. The minimal test set must include partial paths BC or BD, CE,
       DE, FG or F..K, GH, H..J or H..K, JK, AB, and AF. This can be done with
       any C1 test set.

See Fig. 10-5.

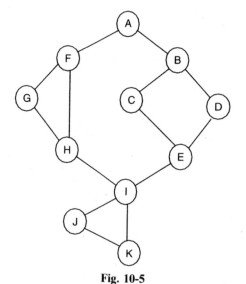

Fig. 10-5

CHAPTER 11

Object-Oriented Development

11.1   Introduction

Object-oriented software is different than conventional software. There are potentially many benefits to object-oriented development. Among these benefits are simplification of requirements, design, and implementation. These benefits are achieved by modeling the problem domain with objects that represent the important entities, by encapsulating the functions with the data, by reusing objects within a project and between projects, and by having a solution that is much closer intellectually[1] to the problem.

The Unified Modeling Language (UML) is the standard notation for object-oriented models. The specification of the UML is available on the Web.[2]

11.1.1   INHERITANCE

One of the innovative ideas in object-oriented software is *inheritance*. Inheritance comes from the recognition of the hierarchy of ideas and concepts, and how this hierarchy/classification involves much inherent reuse of ideas and so on from the higher-level concepts to the lower-level specialization of those concepts.

When two groups of entities are related by one being a specialization of the other, there is the potential for an inheritance relationship. In an inheritance

---

[1] Intellectual distance is a term used to describe how close two ideas are to each other—in this case, how close the structure of the real-world problem is to the structure of the solution.

[2] www.omg.org, or search with the keyword "UML."

relationship, the base class (the more general class) will contain all common attributes. The derived class (the more specialized class) will inherit all the common attributes from the base class.

For example, if one group of entities consists of vehicles and the other group of cars, we can use inheritance. The cars can inherit from the vehicles. The cars can share many of the attributes and operations of the vehicle class. All the common attributes can be located in the base class. The derived class will automatically inherit those attributes. This sharing saves effort.

EXAMPLE 11.1
Draw an object model that identifies all the commonalities between cars and vehicles.

Fig. 11-1 shows that cars and vehicles both have bodies, engines, wheels (maybe not four), headlights, brand names, manufacturer, and cost. (There are probably many more.)

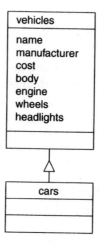

Fig. 11-1

EXAMPLE 11.2
Draw an object model that identifies the commonalities in a library system that handles books, magazines, pamphlets, movie videotapes, music CDs, audio book tapes, and newspapers.

Figure 11-2 shows that all of these items have titles, publishers, acquisition dates, catalog numbers, shelf location, loan status, and checkout limits.

Some example attributes have been added to some of the derived classes. Note that audiobook could be derived from book, and newspaper and magazine could both be derived from an object called serial or periodical.

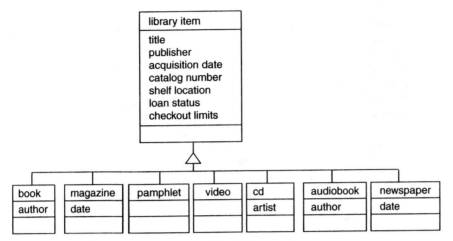

Fig. 11-2

11.1.2 POLYMORPHISM

Polymorphism means "able to assume many forms." It refers to functions that can deal with different versions or forms of the object or parameter list. In object-oriented software, it often means a function that can deal with the base type or a derived type. In the car/vehicle example, the base class will have polymorphic functions for tasks that all vehicles perform but may perform differently, such as turn corners. Each derived class will either use the base class function or provide a version that is suitable for the derived class.

> **EXAMPLE 11.3**
> Find the functions in the library problem (Example 11.2) that can be common for all of the items and the functions that will have to be specialized for the derived class.
>   *Common*—Checkout and check in functions (except maybe for checkout limitations).
>   *Specialized*—Cataloging functions will differ.

11.2   Identifying Objects

One approach to identifying the requirements of a proposed system is to start with identifying the objects in the problem domain. These objects are usually nouns in the problem statement.

11.2.1 THE NOUN-IN-TEXT APPROACH

In the *noun-in-text* approach, all the nouns in the text are identified. Different nouns may be used for the same concept. These equivalent nouns and nouns associated with each concept should be sorted into groups. Some nouns will be related to the environment outside of the proposed system and may be removed.

In each group, nouns representing the objects should be selected. Other nouns in the group may become attributes or may be discarded.

EXAMPLE 11.4

Use the noun-in-text-description method to identify the objects from the following grocery store problem:

> A grocery store wants to automate its inventory. It has point-of-sale terminals that can record all of the items and quantities that a customer purchases. It has a similar terminal for the customer service desk to handle returns. It has another terminal in the loading dock to handle arriving shipments from suppliers. The meat department and the produce departments have terminals to enter losses/discounts due to spoilage.

Nouns:

grocery store, inventory, point-of-sale terminals, items, quantities, customer, purchases, service desk, returns, loading dock, shipments, suppliers, meat department, produce department, losses, discounts

Groups:

grocery store
inventory, items, quantities, returns, losses, discounts
shipments
suppliers
meat department, produce department
customers

Environment entities that are external to system:
point-of-sale terminals, service desk, loading dock, meat department, produce department

However, meat items and produce items should be included to reflect the different processing.

There is a choice of whether customers are external to the system or the system knows and tracks customers. The decision is made to track customers.

Final list of objects and attributes:

```
grocery store
inventory
items with an attribute of quantity
customer
purchases
returns
shipments
suppliers
losses
discounts
meat items
produce items
```

See Fig. 11-3.

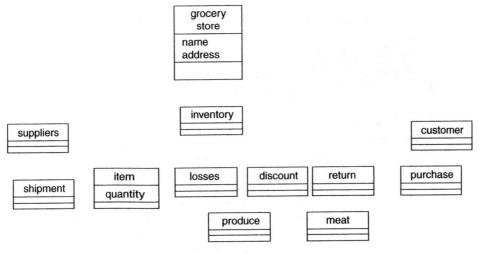

Fig. 11-3

EXAMPLE 11.5
Use the noun-in-text-description method to identify the objects from the following family tree problem:

> Fred is studying genealogy and wants to build a program to store the information that he finds out about his family. He comes from a large family and has lots of uncles, aunts, and cousins.

It is not easy to apply the noun-in-text method to this example. The first sentence is motivation and only the noun "family" is relevant. The second sentence repeats the noun "family" and then lists nouns that are relationships between people. Unlike the previous example, these relations are not derived classes. An uncle is not a specialization of person; it is a relationship between persons.

Familiarity with the problem domain will be necessary to identify the objects. The good set of objects for this problem is family tree, person, and family. See Fig. 11-4.

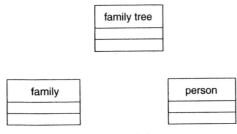

Fig. 11-4

11.2.2   IDENTIFYING INHERITANCE

Inheritance is the "a-kind-of" relationship. The base class is the common object and the derived classes are the specialized instances of the common object. A top-down approach is to identify objects that sometimes take special processing or sometimes have special attributes. This is usually an effective approach to finding inheritance.

The opposite approach is also sometimes useful. It is a bottom-up approach, which is to group all similar items and look for the commonality. The intersection of all the similar items will become the base class.

EXAMPLE 11.6

Identify the possible inheritance in the grocery store (Example 11.4).

A top-down approach would help to realize that the meat department and the produce department have special processing of the items. This would lead to a base class of items and derived classes of meat and produce. An expert in the domain of grocery stores could help to identify all the other derived classes that can occur in a grocery store.

Additionally, a bottom-up approach would find the commonality among the objects `losses`, `discount`, `return`, and `purchase`. This suggests that those objects can be derived from an object `transaction`. See Fig. 11-5.

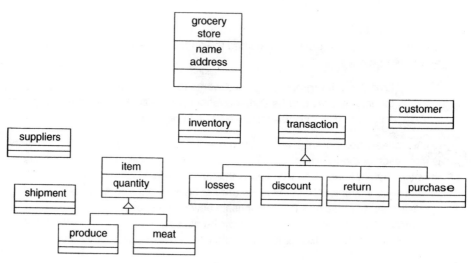

Fig. 11-5

11.2.3   IDENTIFYING REUSE

Reuse is one of the promises of object-oriented software. However, reuse rarely happens by itself. The first step in identifying reuse is a task called domain analysis. ***Domain analysis*** is the process of reviewing the problem domain to determining what objects and functions are common to all activities. Without good domain knowledge, it will be hard to identify what commonalities exist between all similar systems in that domain. For reuse to be effective, the parts that will be useful in multiple solutions in that domain must be identified. This means understanding the potential commonalities.

Approaches to reuse can be top-down or bottom-up. Bottom-up approaches look for low- or middle-level classes that will be common in most solutions in that domain. Top-down approaches see the commonality in the framework of the solution and the differences in the low-level objects.

Unless reuse is a goal and identifying potential reuse and designing classes to be reusable is a top priority, reuse will be elusive.

> **EXAMPLE 11.7**
> Identify reuse in the grocery store domain (Examples 11.4 and 11.6).
> In the domain of grocery stores, it would seem that the commonality was in the low-level objects. Most grocery stores handle the same sort of items. Some middle-level activities would have a lot of commonality, for example, inventory systems, stocking, and tracking sales.

11.2.4 USE CASE APPROACH

Another approach to identifying the requirements of a proposed system is to start with identifying the scenarios. This approach views the activities as the best way to determine the necessary functionality and the objects needed to support that functionality.

> **EXAMPLE 11.8**
> Write scenarios for the grocery store problem (Example 11.7). Develop a list of objects from the scenarios.
> Most of the scenarios will be based on general domain knowledge and are not derivable just from the short problem statement.
> **Scenario 1**: The inventory is running low; the supplier is sent an order; the order arrives at the shipping dock; the items and quantities are entered into the inventory.
> **Scenario 2**: The customer buys groceries and checks out; the customer database is updated (the decision again is made to have the system track customers).
> **Scenario 3**: A new customer enters the store and is asked to fill out a new customer information form and receives the membership card.
> **Scenario 4**: The produce clerk inspects the produce and throws away the old lettuce; the inventory is updated.
> From these scenarios, we can easily identify the following objects:
>
> ```
> inventory, supplier, order, shipment, items, customer, membership
>                     card, produce item
> ```
>
> The inheritance relation between grocery item (base class) and produce item (derived class) is clear.

11.3 Identifying Associations

After the objects in a domain are identified, the next step is to identify the associations between the objects. An association denotes a relationship between two objects. The different kinds of associations were described in Section 2.4. An association between objects means that in the implementation of the system, there will be a link between the objects. Thus, the importance of the associations is that the associations determine what access an object has to other objects. This access is essential to efficient implementation of functionality.

There are different approaches for determining the associations between objects. One approach is to identify the associations that exist in the problem domain.

EXAMPLE 11.9

Develop associations for the family tree problem of Example 11.5.

The problem statement mentions aunts, uncles, and cousins. These are all associations (relationships). They are not the primitive associations. The basic associations in genealogy are mother, father, and child. The inverse of each of these associations is marriage, marriage, and birthfamily, respectively.

Additionally, there is an association (aggregation) from the top object, family-tree, to marriage and to person. These can be called marriages and people, respectively. See Fig. 11-6.

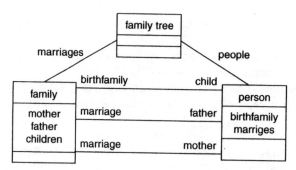

Fig. 11-6

Another approach to identifying associations is to think about the functionality that is required. If one object is required to have functionality that requires access to other objects, then an association, or a sequence of associations, must exist between those objects.

EXAMPLE 11.10

A college wants a system that handles the courses, sections of courses, and students. Draw an object model and identify the associations between the objects.

The college will need to access the students for printing out student information. To print out courses taken by students, there needs to be access from students to sections. To print out the line schedule that prints the sections that are available, there needs to be access to courses and then to sections for each course. See Fig. 11-7.

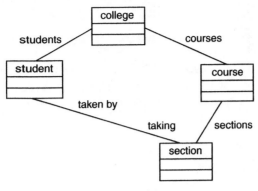

Fig. 11-7

11.3.1   EXISTENCE DEPENDENCY

Another approach is to use the existence dependency (Section 2.4.1) relationship between objects to determine the required associations. Two objects have an existence dependency relationship if the existence of the child object is dependent on exactly one instance of the parent object. This means that the parent instance exists before the child instance is created and the child instance is deleted before the parent instance is deleted.

> **EXAMPLE 11.11**
> Use existence dependency to structure the associations in the library example, Example 2.6.
>   Neither book nor person is existence dependent on library. However, their participation in the library in terms of patron and copy, respectively, does satisfy the existence dependency requirements. See Fig. 11-8.

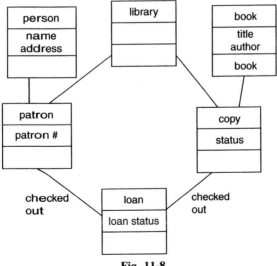

Fig. 11-8

EXAMPLE 11.12
Use existence dependency to determine the association in the student section problem of Example 11.10.

The object model developed in Example 11.10 does not satisfy the existence dependency rules, since `section` cannot be existence dependent on `student` or vice versa. Thus, an additional object called `enrollment` must be used. See Fig. 11-9.

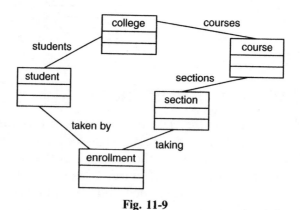

Fig. 11-9

11.4   Identifying Multiplicities

Multiplicities are restrictions on the associations between instances of objects. The multiplicity is specified by an expression at the end of the association. The expression can be a single value, a range of values, or a list of ranges or single values. In the range, the two values are separated by two periods.

The problem domain often has restrictions on how many relationships an instance of an object can have with instances of other objects.

EXAMPLE 11.13
Use multiplicities to restrict how many times a copy of a book can be borrowed at a given time.

As shown in Fig. 11-10 the 0..1 at the loan end of the association restricts a copy to be participating in at most one loan relationship at a time. The 1 at the copy end of the association requires a loan to have exactly one association with a copy. That is, there cannot be a loan without exactly one copy associated with the loan.

The check-out association restricts the loan instance to be associated with exactly one patron. The patron can have the association with zero or more loan instances.

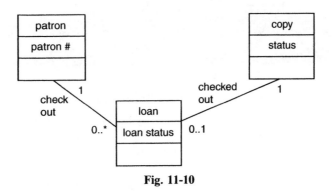

Fig. 11-10

EXAMPLE 11.14
Determine the multiplicities for the student-section problem from Example 11.12.
   All instances have to be related to exactly one parent instance. All parents have to be related to 1 to n child instances. For example, a college without courses is not allowed (by this model). For example, 0..*, specifies that there can be zero or more relationships. And, every course has to be associated with one college.
   See Fig. 11-11.

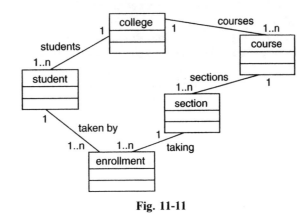

Fig. 11-11

Review Questions

1. Why is a Ford automobile a specialization of a car and an engine is not?
2. What is the difference between an object and an attribute?
3. What are the goals of domain analysis?

Problems

1. Identify the objects from the following B&B problem statement:

Tom and Sue are starting a bed-and-breakfast in a small New England town. They will have three bedrooms for guests. They want a system to manage the reservations and to monitor expenses and profits. When a potential customer calls for a reservation, they will check the calendar, and if there is a vacancy, they will enter the customer name, address, phone number, dates, agreed upon price, credit card number, and room number(s). Reservations must be guaranteed by 1 day's payment.

Reservations will be held without guarantee for an agreed upon time. If not guaranteed by that date, the reservation will be dropped.

2. Identify the objects from the following dental office problem statement:

Tom is starting a dental practice in a small town. He will have a dental assistant, a dental hygienist, and a receptionist. He wants a system to manage the appointments.

When a patient calls for an appointment, the receptionist will check the calendar and will try to schedule the patient as early as possible to fill in vacancies. If the patient is happy with the proposed appointment, the receptionist will enter the appointment with patient name and purpose of appointment. The system will verify the patient name and supply necessary details from the patient records including the patient's ID number. After each exam or cleaning, the hygienist or assistant will mark the appointment as completed, add comments, and then schedule the patient for the next visit if appropriate.

The system will answer queries by patient name and by date. Supporting details from the patient's records are displayed along with the appointment information. The receptionist can cancel appointments. The receptionist can print out a notification list for making reminder calls 2 days before appointments. The system includes the patient's phone numbers from the patient records. The receptionist can also print out daily and weekly work schedules with all the patients.

3. Draw an object model for the B&B problem (Problem 11.1).

4. Draw an object model for the dental office problem (Problem 11.2).

Answers to Review Questions

1. Why is a Ford automobile a specialization of a car and an engine is not?

A Ford automobile would have the same attributes and functions that a base class for cars would have. Thus, a Ford automobile could be derived from that `car` base class.

However, an engine is a part of a car and not a specialization of a car. There are many functions and attributes of cars that an engine would not have. Thus, an engine could not be derived from a `car` base class.

2. What is the difference between an object and an attribute?

An object is an entity, while an attribute is a characteristic of that object. For example, a person would be an object and the person's height would be an attribute. Sometimes the distinction may be hard. In the person/height example, person may be a base class and there may be derived classes for tall person, short person, and medium-height person.

3. What is the goal of domain analysis?

The goal of domain analysis is to identify the parts that would be best to reuse in future systems. The approach is to find commonality among possible systems in the problem domain.

Answers to Problems

1. Identify the objects from the B&B problem statement.

Objects

```
bed-and-breakfast
bedroom
reservation
calendar
customer
guarantee
payment
expense
```

2. Identify the objects from the dental office problem statement.

Objects

```
dental office
patients
appointments
calendar
patient records
notification list
daily work schedule
weekly work schedule
```

3. Draw an object model for the B&B problem.
See Fig. 11-12.

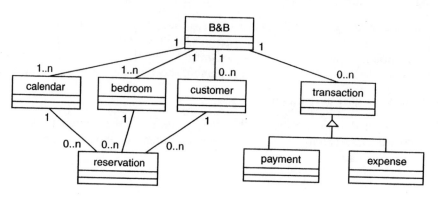

Fig. 11-12. B&B object model.

4. Draw an object model for the dental problem.

See Fig. 11-13.

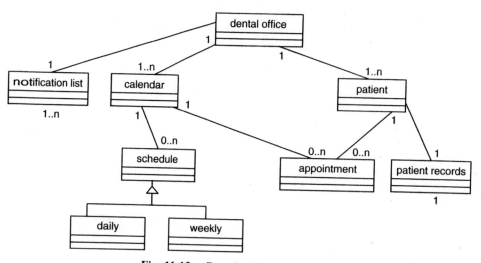

Fig. 11-13. Dental office object model.

CHAPTER 12

Object-Oriented Metrics

12.1   Introduction

The measurement of object-oriented software has the same goals (see Chapter 5) as the measurement of conventional software: trying to understand the characteristics of the software. *Object-oriented* refers to a programming language and programming style where the functions are encapsulated with the data. The encapsulation is accomplished by limiting the accessibility to the data to functions that ensure the integrity of the data. Additionally, object-oriented software involves inheritance and dynamic binding. Object-oriented software is suppose to model the real world and thus be easier to understand, easier to modify (maintain), and easier to reuse. However, much of the complexity of object-oriented software is not evident in the static structure of the source code. The area of object-oriented software measurement is a research area.

The metrics presented in Sections 12.2 and 12.3 are the current view of what is significant. Chidamber and Kemerer proposed the metrics in Section 12.2.[1] Section 12.3 presents the MOOD metrics.[2] Much further work will be necessary before there is consensus of which object-oriented metrics are useful.

12.1.1   TRADITIONAL MEASUREMENT

Measures from traditional software measurement could be applied. This might be useful within large functions. However, software measurement for non-object-oriented software uses the control flow graph (and variations such as the data flow graph) as the basic abstraction of the software. The control flow graph does not appear to be useful as an abstraction of object-oriented software. Little work

---

1 Shyam Chidamber and Chris Kemerer, "A Metrics Suite for Object Oriented Design," *IEEE TOSE* (Transactions on Software Engineering) 20:6 June 1994, 476–493.

2 Rachel Harrison, Steve Counsell, and Reuben Nithi, "An Evaluation of the MOOD Set of Object-Oriented Software Metrics," *IEEE TOSE* 24:6 June 1998, 491–496.

has been published evaluating the use of McCabe's cyclomatic number or Halstead's software science in object-oriented software development. The intuitive problem with applying the traditional software metrics is that the complexity of object-oriented software does not appear to be in the control structure.

12.1.2   OBJECT-ORIENTED ABSTRACTIONS

In most object-oriented software, the methods are small and the number of decisions in a method is often small. Most of the complexity appears to be in the calling patterns among the methods. There has been little work in this area, and there is little agreement on which abstractions are significant. The more common abstractions in object-oriented software development are the diagrams used in the Unified Modeling Language (UML).

12.2   Metrics Suite for Object-Oriented Design

The Metric Suite for Object-Oriented Design is intended to be a comprehensive approach to evaluating the classes in a system. Most of these are calculated on a per class basis. That is, none of these evaluate the system as a whole. It is not clear how to extend these metrics to the whole system. Averaging them over the classes in a system is usually not appropriate.

12.2.1   METRIC 1: WEIGHTED METHODS PER CLASS (WMC)

The *weighted methods per class* metric is based on the intuition that the number of methods per class is a significant indication of the complexity of the software. Further consideration may be necessary to avoid giving full weight to trivial methods, for example, get and set methods. The WMC includes the provision for weighting the methods. Let C be a set of classes each with the number of methods $M_1, \ldots, M_n$. Let $c_1, \ldots, c_n$ be the complexity (weights) of the classes (the value that is to be used for c_i is not defined in the paper).

$$\text{WMC} = \frac{1}{n} * \sum_{i=0}^{n} c_i * M_i$$

This is the only metric in the suite that is averaged over the classes in a system. In the examples, we will assume c_i is equal to 1.

12.2.2   METRIC 2: DEPTH OF INHERITANCE TREE (DIT)

The *depth of inheritance tree* metric is just the maximum length from any node to the root of the inheritance tree for that class. Inheritance can add to complexity of software. This metric is calculated for each class.

12.2.3   METRIC 3: NUMBER OF CHILDREN (NOC)

Not only is the depth of the inheritance tree significant, but the width of the inheritance tree. The **number of children** metric is the number of immediate subclasses subordinated to a class in the inheritance hierarchy. This metric is calculated for each class.

12.2.4   METRIC 4: COUPLING BETWEEN OBJECT CLASSES (CBO)

Coupling between modules has always been a concern (see Section 9.5). In object-oriented software, we can define **coupling** as the use of methods or attributes in another class. Two classes will be considered coupled when methods declared in one class use methods or instance variables defined by the other class. Coupling is symmetric. If class A is coupled to class B, then B is coupled to A. The **coupling between object classes** (CBO) metric will be the count of the number of other classes to which it is coupled.

This metric is calculated for each class.

12.2.5   METRIC 5: RESPONSE FOR A CLASS (RFC)

The **response set of a class**, {RS}, is the set of methods that can potentially be executed in response to a message received by an object of that class. It is the union of all methods in the class and all methods called by methods in the class. It is only counted on one level of call.

$$RFC = |RS|$$

This metric is calculated for each class.

12.2.6   METRIC 6: LACK OF COHESION IN METHODS (LCOM)

A module (or class) is cohesive if everything is closely related. The lack of cohesion in methods metric tries to measure the lack of cohesiveness.

Let I_i be the set of instance variables used by method i.
Let P be set of pairwise null intersections of I_i.
Let Q be set of pairwise nonnull intersections.

The LCOM metric can be visualized by considering a bipartite graph. One set of nodes consists of the attributes, and the other set of nodes consists of the functions. An attribute is linked to a function if that function accesses or sets that attribute. The set of arcs is the set Q. If there are n attributes and m functions, then there are a possible $n * m$ arcs. So, the size of P is $n * m$ minus the size of Q.

$$LCOM = max(|P| - |Q|, 0)$$

This metric is calculated on a class basis.

EXAMPLE 12.1

Calculate the Chidamber suite of metrics on the following example C++ program that provides a link list of rectangles:

```cpp
class point {
   float x;
   float y;
public:
   point(float newx, float newy) {x=newx; y=newy;}
   getx(){return x;}
   gety(){return y;}
};
class rectangle {
   point pt1, pt2, pt3, pt4;
public:
   rectangle(float pt1x, pt1y, pt2x, pt2y, pt3x, pt3y, pt4x, pt4y)
      { pt1 = new point(pt1x, pt1y); pt2 = new point(pt2x, pt2y);
       pt3 = new point(pt3x, pt3y); pt4 = new point(pt4x, pt4y);}
   float length(point r, point s){return sqrt((r.getx()-s.getx())^2+
       (r.gety()-s.gety())^2); }
   float area(){return length(pt1,pt2) * length(pt1,pt3);}
};
class linklistnode {
   rectangle* node;
   linklistnode* next;
public:
   linklistnode(rectangle* newRectangle){node=newRectangle; next=0;}
   linklistnode* getNext(){return next;}
   rectangle* getRectangle(){return node;}
   void setnext(linklistnode* newnext){next=newnext;}
};
class rectanglelist {
   linklistnode* top;
public:
   rectanglelist(){top = 0;}
   void addRectangle(float x1, y1, x2, y2, x3, y3, x4, y4) {
      linklistnode* tempLinkListNode; rectangle* tempRectangle;
      tempRectangle = new rectangle(x1,y1,x2,y2,x3,y3,x4,y4);
      tempLinkListNode = new linkListNode(tempRectangle);
      tempLinkListNode->setnext(top);
      top=tempLinkListNode; }
   float totalArea(){float sum; sum=0; linklistnode* temp; temp=top;
      while (temp !=0){sum=sum + temp->getRectangle()->area();
        temp=temp->getNext();}
      return sum;}
};
```

Metric 1: Weighted Methods per Class

Class	# Methods
point	3
rectangle	3
linklistnode	4
rectanglelist	3

$$\text{WMC} = 13/4 = 3.25 \text{ methods/class}$$

Metric 2: Depth of Inheritance Tree (DIT)

There is no inheritance in this example.

Metric 3: Number of Children (NOC)

There is no inheritance in this example.

Metric 4: Coupling between Object Classes (CBO)

See Fig. 12-1.

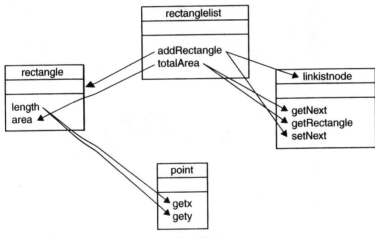

Fig. 12-1

The class diagram is annotated with arrows to show which functions (or constructors) are called by each function (only calls in other classes are shown).

Class	Coupled Classes	CBO
point	rectangle	1
rectangle	point, rectanglelist	2
linklistnode	rectanglelist	1
rectanglelist	rectangle, linklistnode	2

Metric 5: Response for a Class (RFC)

Class	Response Set	RFC
point	point, getx, gety	3
rectangle	rectangle, point, length, getx, gety, area	6
linklistnode	linkListNode, getNext, getRectangle, setNext	4
rectanglelist	rectangleList, addRectangle, rectangle, setNext totalArea, getRectangle, area, getNext	8

Metric 6: Lack of Cohesion in Methods (LCOM)
See Fig. 12-2.

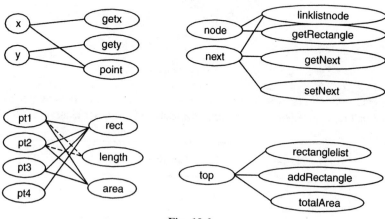

Fig. 12-2

The lines between length and the points are dashed because it depends on the parameters as to which ones are actually accessed on a specific call.

Class	LCOM
`point`	$\max(0,(6-4)-4)=0$
`rectangle`	$\max(0,(12-9)-9)=0$
`linklistnode`	$\max(0,(8-5)-5)=0$
`rectanglelist`	$\max(0,(3-3)-3)=0$

12.3   The MOOD Metrics

The MOOD (see page 183) suite of metrics is also intended as a complete set that measures the attributes of encapsulation, inheritance, coupling, and polymorphism of a system.

Let TC be the total number of classes in the system.

Let $M_d(C_i)$ be the number of methods declared in a class.

Consider the predicate Is_visible($M_{m,i}$, C_j), where $M_{m,i}$ is the method m in class i and Cj is the class j. This predicate is 1 if $i \mathrel{!}= j$ and Cj may call $M_{m,i}$. Otherwise, the predicate is 0. For example, a public method in C++ is visible to all other classes. A private method in C++ is not visible to other classes.

The visibility, $V(M_{m,i})$, of a method, $M_{m,i}$, is defined as follows:

$$V(M_{m,i}) = \frac{\sum_{j=1}^{TC} \text{Is\_visible}(M_{m,i}, C_j)}{TC - 1}$$

12.3.1   ENCAPSULATION

The *method hiding factor* (MHF) and the *attribute hiding factor* (AHF) attempt to measure the encapsulation.

$$\text{MHF} = \frac{\sum_{i=1}^{TC} \sum_{m=1}^{M_d(C_i)} (1 - V(M_{m,i}))}{\sum_{i=1}^{TC} M_d(C_i)}$$

$$\text{AHF} = \frac{\sum_{i=1}^{TC} \sum_{m=1}^{A_d(C_i)} (1 - V(A_{m,i}))}{\sum_{i=1}^{TC} A_d(C_i)}$$

EXAMPLE 12.2

Calculate MHF and AHF for the following C++ code:

```
Class A{
    int a;
public:
    void x();
    void y();
};
Class B {
    int b;
    int bb;
    void w();
public:
    void z():
};
Class C {
    int c;
    void v();
};
TC = 3
```

method	is_vis(A)	is_vis(B)	is_vis(C)	$V(M_{m,i})$
A::x()	0	1	1	1
A::y()	0	1	1	1
B::w()	0	0	0	0
B::z()	1	0	1	1
C::v()	0	0	0	0

MHF = 2/5 = 0.4

attribute	is_vis(A)	is_vis(B)	is_vis(C)	$V(A_{m,i})$
A::a()	0	0	0	0
B::b()	0	0	0	0
B::bb()	0	0	0	0
C::c()	0	0	0	0

AHF = 4/4 = 1.0

12.3.2   INHERITANCE FACTORS

There are two measures of the inheritance, the ***method inheritance factor*** (MIF) and the ***attribute inheritance factor*** (AIF).

$M_d(C_i)$ = Number of methods declared in a class i
$M_i(C_i)$ = Number of methods inherited (and not overridden) in a class i
$M_a(C_i) = M_d(C_i) + M_i(C_i)$ = Number of methods that can be invoked in association with class i

$$\text{MIF} = \frac{\sum_{i=1}^{TC} M_i(C_i)}{\sum_{i=1}^{TC} M_a(C_i)}$$

$A_d(C_i)$ = Number of attributes declared in a class i
$A_i(C_i)$ = Number of attributes from base classes that are accessible in a class i
$A_a(C_i) = A_d(C_i) + A_i(C_i)$ = Number of attributes that can be accessed in association with class i

$$\text{AIF} = \frac{\sum_{i=1}^{TC} A_i(C_i)}{\sum_{i=1}^{TC} A_a(C_i)}$$

EXAMPLE 12.3

Calculate MIF and AIF from the following C++ code:

```
Class A{
protected:
   int a;
public:
   void x();
   virtual void y();
};
Class B public A {
   int b;
protected:
   int bb;
public:
   void z():
   void y();
   void w();
};
Class C public B {
   int c;
   void v();
};
```

class	Md	Mi	Ad	Ai
A	x(),y()	none	a	none
B	w(),z(),y()	A::x()	b,bb	A::a
C	v()	B::w(),z(),y	c	B::bb
		A::x()		

MIF = 5/11 AIF = 2/6

12.3.3   COUPLING FACTOR

The *coupling factor* (CF) measures the coupling between classes excluding coupling due to inheritance.

Let is_client(c_i,c_j) = 1 if class i has a relation with class j; otherwise, it is zero. The relation might be that class i calls a method in class j or has a reference to class j or to an attribute in class j. This relationship cannot be inheritance.

$$CF = \frac{\sum_{i=1}^{TC} \sum_{j=1}^{TC} is\_client(c_i, c_j)}{TC^2 - TC}$$

EXAMPLE 12.4

Calculate the coupling factor on the object model shown in Fig. 12-3 for the bed-and-breakfast problem (Problem 11.4). Only assume a relationship if it is required by the associations shown on the diagram.

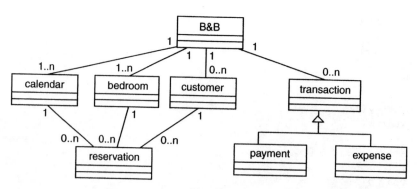

Fig. 12-3

$$TC = 7$$

Class	is_client classes
B&B	calendar, bedroom, customer, transaction
calendar	reservation
bedroom	reservation
customer	reservation
transaction	none
payment	none
expense	none

$$CF = 7/42$$

12.3.4   POLYMORPHISM FACTOR

The *polymorphism factor* (PF) is a measure of the potential for polymorphism.

Let $M_o(C_i)$ be the number of overriding methods in class i.
Let $M_n(C_i)$ be the number of new methods in class i.
Let $DC(C_i)$ be the number of descendants of class i.

$$PF = \frac{\sum_{i=1}^{TC} M_o(C_i)}{\sum_{i=1}^{TC}[M_n(C_i) \times DC(C_i)]}$$

EXAMPLE 12.5
Calculate the polymorphism factor on the C++ code from Example 12.3.

Class	Mn	Mo	DC
A	x(),y()	none	2
B	w(),z()	y()	1
C	v()	none	0

$$PF = 1/(2*2+2*1+1*0) = 1/6$$

Review Questions

1. Why are McCabe's cyclomatic number and Halstead's software science not readily applicable to object-oriented software?
2. What abstractions are available in object-oriented design to be used as the basis of object-oriented metrics?
3. When should a metric for a whole system be different than either the sum or the average of metrics calculated for each class?
4. Is a high LCOM good or bad?
5. Some people have suggested that, in LCOM, just using the difference between the size of P and Q. That is, the use of the maximum of zero and this difference is not effective. What would be the effect of this change?

Problems

1. Calculate the Chidamber metrics for the following code that maintains an array of people/students:

```
class person{
   char* name;
   char* ssn;
public:
   person(){name = new char[NAMELENGTH]; ssn = new
      char[SSNLENGTH];}
   ~person(){delete name; delete ssn;}
   void addName(char* newname){strcpy(name, newname);}
   void addSsn(char* newssn){strcpy(ssn, newssn);}
   char* getName(){return name;}
   void virtual display(){cout << "the person's name is
      "<<name;}
};
class student public person {
   float gpa;
public:
   void addGpa(float newgpa){gpa = newgpa;}
   void display(){cout<<"the student's name is"
   <<getName()<<" and gpa is " << gpa;}

};
```

```
class personlist {
  person* list[MAX];
  int listIndex;
public:
  personlist(){listIndex = 0;}
  void addPerson(char* newname, char*
  newssn){list[listIndex]=new person;
    list[listIndex]->addName(newname); list[listIndex]
    ->addSsn(newssn);
    listIndex++; }
  void addStudent(char* newname, char* newssn, float gpa)
    {student* temp = new student;
    temp->addName(newname); temp->addSsn(newssn);
    temp->addGpa(newgpa);list[listIndex++]=temp;}
  void display() { int j; for(j=0; j<listIndex; j++) list[j]
  ->display();}
};
```

Answers to Review Questions

1. Why are McCabe's cyclomatic number and Halstead's software science not readily applicable to object-oriented software?

These two metrics are based on the size and complexity of an algorithm written as a single function. Object-oriented functions are usually spread over a number of methods, often in different classes. Each object-oriented function is often small and relatively simple. Thus, these two metrics will probably not give a good measure of the complexity of the object-oriented system.

2. What abstractions are available in object-oriented design to be used as the basis of object-oriented metrics?

The standard abstractions are the UML diagrams: object models, use case diagrams, state models, and sequence diagrams. None of these appear to capture the essential notion of complexity in object-oriented software.

3. When should a metric for a whole system be different than either the sum or the average of metrics calculated for each class?

If the metric for the individual class is basically a size metric, such as LOC or number of children, then it would make sense to sum those individual metric values to obtain a metric value for the whole system or an average size per class. If the individual class metric was an average, then an average of the averages might be reasonable—for instance, the average number of parameters per function.

However, neither the sum nor the average will be a good metric of the interactions between classes.

4. Is a high LCOM good or bad?

Bad, since it implies a high lack of cohesion.

5. Some people have suggested that, in LCOM, just using the difference between the size of P and Q. That is, the use of maximum of zero and this difference is not effective. What would be the effect of this change?

It would allow discrimination between the more cohesive classes. Now a cohesive class just maps to zero.

 ## Answers to Problem

1. Calculate the Chidamber metrics for the code from the problem statement that maintains an array of people/students.

Metric 1: Weighted Methods per Class

Class	# Methods
person	6
student	2
personlist	4

Note that the inherited functions were not counted.

$$WMC = 12/3 = 4 \text{ methods/class}$$

Metric 2: Depth of Inheritance Tree (DIT)

Class	DIT
person	0
student	1
personlist	0

Metric 3: Number of Children (NOC)

Class	NOC
person	1
student	0
personlist	0

Metric 4: Coupling between Object Classes (CBO)

See Fig. 12-4.

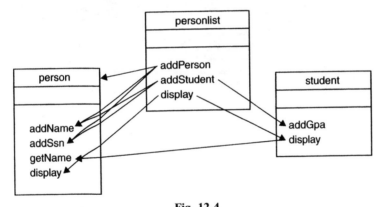

Fig. 12-4

The class diagram is annotated with arrows to show which functions (or constructors) are called by each function (only calls in other classes are shown).

Class	Coupled Classes	CBO
person	student, personlist	2
student	person, personlist	2
personlist	person, student	2

Metric 5: Response for a Class (RFC)

Class	Response Set	RFC
person	person, addName, addSssm getName, display	5
student	student, addGpa, person, getName	6
personlist	personlist, addPerson, addStudent, addName, addSsn, addGpa, display	7

Metric 6: Lack of Cohesion in Methods (LCOM)

See Fig. 12-5.

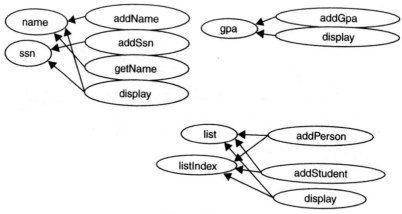

Fig. 12-5

Class	LCOM
person	$\max(0,(8-5)-5)=0$
student	$\max(0,(2-2)-2)=0$
personlist	$\max(0,(6-6)-6)=0$

CHAPTER 13

Object-Oriented Testing

13.1   Introduction

Testing object-oriented software presents some new challenges. Many conventional techniques are still appropriate. For example, functional testing of object-oriented software will be no different from functional testing of conventional software. Test cases will be developed based on the required functionality as described in the requirement documentation. However, structural testing of object-oriented software will be very different. Two structural testing approaches will be covered: *MM testing* and **function pair** testing

Conventional Software

The testing of conventional software is often based on coverage criteria defined on the structure of the software. The standard approaches (see Chapter 10) include statement coverage, branch coverage, and data flow coverage. These coverage criteria are based on the control flow diagram or a modified control flow diagram.

Object-Oriented Software

Object-oriented software adds a new complexity to software testing. The control flow diagram is no longer a good representation of the structure of the software. It would be more appropriate to base structural testing on an object model. However, no effective coverage measures of object models have been found.

The methods in the class should be tested with the techniques already presented. The same coverage criteria can be applied to object-oriented software. Intuitively, however, the statement and branch coverage criteria do not seem appropriate for thoroughly testing the complexities of object-oriented software. The interactions between methods need to be tested.

One approach to object-oriented testing is to cover all the calls to methods. This is sometimes called **MM** testing.

13.2   MM Testing

The *MM testing* (method-message) coverage requires that every method call be tested. Thus, in every method, every call to another method must be tested at least once. If a method calls another method multiple times, each calls needs to be tested only once. This seems to be the most basic coverage criterion. The MM testing does not subsume every-statement coverage (see Section 10.3.1).

EXAMPLE 13.1
Identify the MM testing coverage for the linked list of rectangles problem.

```
class point {
  float x;
  float y;
public:
  point(float newx, float newy) {x=newx; y=newy;}
  getx(){return x;}
  gety(){return y;}
};
class rectangle {
  point pt1, pt2, pt3, pt4;
public:
  rectangle(float pt1x, pt1y, pt2x, pt2y, pt3x, pt3y, pt4x, pt4y)
    { pt1 = new point(pt1x, pt1y); pt2 = new point(pt2x, pt2y);
      pt3 = new point(pt3x, pt3y); pt4 = new point(pt4x, pt4y);}
  float length(point r, point s) {return sqrt((r.getx()-s.getx())^2+
    (r.gety()-s.gety())^2); }
  float area(){return length(pt1,pt2) * length(pt1,pt3);}
};
class linklistnode {
  rectangle* node;
  linklistnode* next;
public:
  linklistnode(rectangle* newRectangle){node=newRectangle; next=0;}
  linklistnode* getNext(){return next;}
  rectangle* getRectangle(){return node;}
  void setnext(linklistnode* newnext){next=newnext;}
};
class rectanglelist {
  linklistnode* top;
public:
  rectanglelist(){top = 0;}
  void addRectangle(float x1, y1, x2, y2, x3, y3, x4, y4) {
    linklistnode* tempLinkListNode; rectangle* tempRectangle;
    tempRectangle = new rectangle(x1,y1,x2,y2,x3,y3,x4,y4);
    tempLinkListNode = new linkListNode(tempRectangle);
    tempLinkListNode->setnext(top);
    top=tempLinkListNode; }
  float totalArea(){float sum; sum=0; linklistnode* temp; temp=top;
    while (temp !=0){sum=sum + temp->getRectangle()->area();
      temp=temp->getNext();}
    return sum;}
};
```

The calling structure is shown in the following. For each class, the functions of that class are listed and then for each function that calls other functions, those called functions are listed. For MM testing, every one of those calls must be executed. For example, four calls to point will be made. No decisions are shown; however, in this program, there are no decisions that affect the calling sequence.

```
class point
  point()
  getx()
  gety()

class rectangle
  rectangle()
    point::point()
    point::point()
    point::point()
    point::point()
  length()
    point::getx()
    point::getx()
    point::gety()
    point::gety()
  area()
    length()
    length()

class linklistnode
  linklistnode()
  getNext()
  getRectangle()
  setnext()
class rectanglelist
  rectanglelist()
  addRectangle()
    rectangle::rectangle()
    linklistnode::linklistnode()
    linklistnode::setnext()
  totalArea()
    linklistnode::getRectangle()
    rectangle::area()
    linklistnode::getNext()
```

MM testing: Any test case that builds at least one rectangle and then gets the total area will execute all of these calls.

13.3　Function Pair Coverage

Function pair coverage requires that for all possible sequences of method executions, those of length two must be tested. This is usually done based on a state machine diagram or on a regular expression showing the possible method executions.

Since a regular expression can be mapped to a finite state machine, these two approaches are equivalent. Although the finite state machine used to describe the behavior of a software system may not be minimal, having additional states will increase the effectiveness of the test set.

EXAMPLE 13.2

Identify the function pair testing coverage for the linked list of rectangles program of Example 13.1. Consider the calling structure of the functions.

```
class point
  point()
  getx()
  gety()

class rectangle
  rectangle()
    point()point()point()point()
  length()
    getx()getx()gety()gety()
  area()
    length()length()

class linklistnode
  linklistnode()
  getNext()
  getRectangle()
  setnext()

class rectanglelist
  rectanglelist()
  addRectangle()
    rectangle()linklistnode()setnext()
  totalArea()
    (getRectangle()area()getNext())*
```

Most of the regular expressions for the individual functions have a fixed list of method calls. Only the `totalArea` function is zero-or-more repetition from the `while` loop.

Putting all of these together into one regular expression and considering that the `rectanglelist` has to be created first and then `addRectangle` or `totalArea` could be done gives the following regular expression:

```
rectanglelist ((addRectangle rectangle point point point point
linklistnode setnext) | (totalArea (getRectangle area length getx getx
gety gety length getx getx gety gety getNext)*)
```

The function pair testing can be achieved by the following test sets:

1. Creating one rectangle, and then calculating the area
2. Creating two or more rectangles, and then calculating the area
3. Not creating any rectangles, and then calculating the area
4. Creating rectangles after calculating the area

EXAMPLE 13.3
Identify the function **pair** testing coverage for the finite stack example shown in the
state machine in Fig. 13-1. The error transitions are shown as arcs without
destination states.

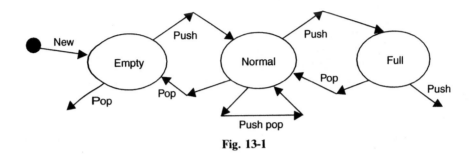

Fig. 13-1

This example would **require** the following pairs in the tests:

1. new pop(on empty − error)
2. new push
3. push (from empty) push
4. push (from empty) pop
5. push (from normal to normal) push (still in normal)
6. push (from normal to normal) push (into full)
7. push (from normal to normal) pop
8. push (from normal to full) push (error)
9. push (from normal to full) pop
10. pop (from normal to normal) push (still in normal)
11. pop (from normal to normal) pop (still in normal)
12. pop (from normal to normal) pop (into empty)
13. pop (into empty) push
14. pop (into empty) pop (error)

EXAMPLE 13.4
Identify the function **pairs** that need to be covered for function pair testing coverage
for the following code **example**. Create the regular expression for each function
that has method calls **within** its body and for the whole program.

```
class D {
   int x;
   int Db(int s) {return 2*s;}
   int Dc(int s) {return s;}
public:
   D(){x=0;}
   int Da(int s){if (x=1) {x=0; return Db(s);} else {x=1; return Dc(s);}}
};
class A {
   int x;
   int y;
   D* m;
public:
   A(){m=new D;}
   virtual int Aa(int s){cout<<x; return m->Da(y);}
```

```
    void add(int s, int u){x=s;y=u;}
};
class B {
  A* w[MAX];
  int z;
  int q;
public:
  B() {z=0; q =1;}
  int Bread(){cin>>s>>u; if (z= MAX) return 0;
    if(s<q){w[z]=new A; w[z]->add(s,u);}
    else {w[z]=new C; w[z]->add(u,s);w[z]->Atadd(s);}
    z++; return z;}
  int Ba(int s){q=w[s]->Aa(q); return q;}
};
class C public A{
  int t;
public:
  int Aa(int r) {cout<<t; return m->Da(t);}
  void Atadd(int x) {t = x;}
};
```

Regular expressions of each function with function calls in its body:

```
class D
  Da : (Db | Dc)
class A
  A: D
  Aa: Da
class B
  Bread: e | (A add | C add Atadd)
  Ba : Aa
class C
  C: A
  Aa: Da
```

Regular expression for possible calls:

```
B (Bread (e | A D add | C A D add Atadd)) | Ba Aa Da (Db | Dc))*
```

The function pair coverage must include the following pairs:

```
B Bread
Bread A
Bread C
Bread Bread
B Ba
Da Db
add Bread
add Ba
Da Dc
Atadd Bread
Atadd Ba
Db Ba
Db Bread
Dc Bread
Dc Ba
```

Review Questions

1. How is functional testing of object-oriented software done?
2. Is statement coverage of object-oriented software useful?
3. Does MM testing subsume statement coverage? (See Section 10.3.1.)
4. What is the advantage of function pair coverage?

Problems

1. Given the following code, generate test cases that satisfy the criteria of MM testing and every function pair testing:

```
class Threes {
  char cout;
public:
  Threes(){count = 'a';}
  void PlusOne() { if(count == 'a') count = 'b'; if(count == 'b')
  count = 'c';
    if(count == 'c') count = 'a'; }
  char* IsDiv() {if(count == 'a'){return 'yes';}else{return
  'no';}}
}
class Num {
  Threes* SumMod3; int last; int number;
  void Digit(int newnum){int j; for (j=1; j<=newnum; j++)
  SumMod3->PlusOne();}
public:
  Num(){SumMod3 = new Threes;}
  void Reduce() {while (number > 0){last = number - (number/
  10)*10;
    Digit(last); number = number/10;}
  char* IsDivisibleBy3(int newnum) {number = newnum; Reduce;
    return SumMod3->IsDiv();}
}
Main() {
  Num* Test = new Num;
  int value;
  char* answer;
  cin >> value;
  answer = test-> IsDivisibleBy3(value);
  cout << answer;
```

Answers to Review Questions

1. How is functional testing of object-oriented software done?

Functional testing of object-oriented software is no different from functional testing of conventional software.

2. Is statement coverage of object-oriented software useful?

Yes, statement coverage of object-oriented software should be done. It is probably the most minimal acceptable coverage.

3. Does MM testing subsume statement coverage? (See Section 10.3.1.)

No, MM testing requires that every method call be tested. However, a section of source code could not contain any method calls and thus not be tested by a set of test cases that achieve MM testing.

4. What is the advantage of function pair coverage?

Function pair coverage ensures that combinations of calls be executed. In the stack example (13.3), if the stack is called by an user interface, there may be only one call of each function. Thus, a simple sequence of create, push, and pop might achieve MM testing. Function pair coverage subsumes MM testing.

Answers to Problems

1. Given the following code, generate test cases that satisfy the criteria of MM testing and every function pair testing:

```
class Threes {
   char cout;
public:
   Threes(){count = 'a';}
   void PlusOne(){ if(count == 'a') count = 'b'; if(count == 'b')
   count = 'c';
     if(count == 'c') count = 'a'; }
   char* IsDiv() {if(count == 'a'){return 'yes';}else{return
   'no';}}
}
class Num {
   Threes* SumMod3; int last; int number;
```

```
    void Digit(int newnum){int j; for (j=1; j<=newnum; j++)
    SumMod3->PlusOne();}
public:
    Num(){SumMod3 = new Threes;}
    void Reduce() {while (number > 0){last = number - (number/
    10)*10;
      Digit(last); number = number/10;}
    char* IsDivisibleBy3(int newnum) {number = newnum; Reduce;
      return SumMod3->IsDiv();}
}
Main() {
    Num* Test = new Num;
    int value;
    char* answer;
    cin >> value;
    answer = test->IsDivisibleBy3(value);
    cout << answer;
```

Regular expressions of calls:

```
    main: Num IsDivisibleBy3
    Num: Threes
    Reduce: Digit *
    IsDivisibleBy3 : Reduce IsDiv
    Digit: PlusOne*
    Threes:
    PlusOne:
    IsDiv
```

MM testing:

The test set must execute all calls.
One test case, input 5—output no, should execute all.

Every function pair:

The test set must have a test for each IsDiv transition, so inputs 6 and 7 should achieve coverage. The outputs are yes and no, respectively.

CHAPTER 14

Formal Notations

14.1   Introduction

A ***formal notation*** is a notation that is mathematically based. Either the syntax and/or the semantics of the notation have a mathematical foundation. Formal notations have tremendous potential for reducing errors during software development. The benefits have not been realized mainly because of the difficulty of constructing and using formal specifications.

The problem with natural language is that it is ambiguous. Often, specifications depend on the semantics/meanings of words to convey the understanding necessary.

Specifications are supposed to answer questions. Any specification, formal or not, can be evaluated as to how well it can answer the developer's questions about the specified behavior. Formal specifications are able to answer the questions more precisely.

There are three levels of formalism:

- ***Informal***—Techniques that have flexible rules that do not constrain the models that can be created
- ***Semiformal***—Techniques that have well-defined syntax
- ***Formal***—Techniques that have rigorously defined syntax and semantics

14.2   Formal specifications

A ***formal specification*** uses a formally defined model to make statements about the software behavior. For example, a formal specification might use set notation as its model. There must be a way to map from the software to the formal model, to relate processes in the software to processes in the formal model, and to map statements in the formal model back to statements in the software.

For example, we could specify the behavior of a stack using the mathematical notation of a sequence. We could specify the mathematical equivalent for each of the stack operations. Then, given a set of operations on the stack, we could map those operations into operations on the mathematical sequence. After completing the operations on the sequence, we could map the result back to the stack. Thus, we could use the mathematical sequence to precisely specify the behavior of the stack.

The statements that are usually made in a formal specification fall into three categories: preconditions, post-conditions, and invariants.

14.2.1   PRECONDITIONS

A *precondition* is a statement associated with a function that must be true before the function can execute. There are two styles of interpreting preconditions:

- *Don't specify error handling*—If the precondition is not met, some error handling is done. This style assumes that the implementation will be extended to handle those error conditions.

- *Specify all error handling*—It is assumed that the function will not be called if the precondition is not met. Thus, the specification is extended to specify all the error conditions that the implemented function will be expected to handle.

14.2.2   POST-CONDITIONS

A post-condition is also associated with a function. The *post-condition* specifies the changes that occur by the completion of the function. Usually, the formal notation has a notation for indicating the situation before the execution and the situation after the execution completes. For example, some notations use an apostrophe to mark the variable to represent the value of the variable after completion, and the variables without an apostrophe represent the values before the function execution starts.

14.2.3   INVARIANTS

An *invariant* is a statement that is always true. Actually, it may not be true during the execution of a function or statement. However, it will be true before and after completion of every function.[1]

An example of an invariant for a stack might be that the stack contains less than or equal to the maximum number of allowed items. Another invariant might be that some field is not null.

---

[1] Even invariants may not be true at all times during actions within a function. For example, an invariant within a loop might state a relationship involving two variables. However, the values of the variables might be updated in two different statements. Between those two statements, the invariant might not be true.

14.3   Object Constraint Language (OCL)

Object Constraint Language (OCL) is part of the UML specification.[2] It was originally used to specify parts of UML. Currently, there is no tool that supports the analysis of OCL statements in the UML specification.

OCL uses the object model to provide the context for the specification. Most OCL statements evaluate to a collection of entities. OCL includes operations and comparisons that can be applied to the resulting collection.

OCL statements are always written with a context. The context is usually a class in the object model. The context is represent by an underlined name of a class.

The OCL expression `self` starts the navigation. It refers to an instance of the class.

14.3.1   NAVIGATION

An OCL expression can use the rolename of the opposite side of an association, the name of the association, or the name of the class. The result will either be a collection or an element. If the multiplicity is 0 or 1, it will be a single object. Otherwise, it will be a collection.

EXAMPLE 14.1
The following OCL statements all evaluate to the set of all loans of books currently borrowed from the library (see object shown in Fig. 14-1).

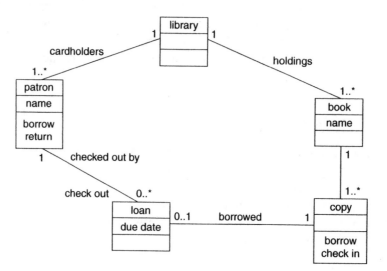

Fig. 14-1

---

[2] The OCL specification is available on the Web. Type "OCL" in a browser search tool or go to www.software.ibm.com/ad/ocl.

```
library
   self.holdings.copy.borrowed
   self.cardholders.checkedout
```

The underlined `library` states the context. The `self` indicates an instance of the class library. The expression `self.holdings` evaluates to the set of all instances of class `book`. The expression `self.holdings.copy` evaluates to the set of all copies of all `books`. The expression `self.holdings.copy.borrowed` evaluates to the set of all instances of `loans` of books from the `library`.

The expression `self.cardholders` evaluates to the set of all instances of `patron`. The expression `self.cardholders.checkedout` evaluates to the set of all instances of `loan`.

14.3.2 INVARIANTS

Invariants in OCL are always written with a context that is shown as an underlined object name. Usually navigation is used to identify a collection or element that is compared with another collection or element. Functions can be applied to the result of the navigation.

EXAMPLE 14.2
Write an invariant for the library problem using the expressions from Example 14.1.

```
library
self.holdings.copy.borrowed = self.cardholders.checkedout
```

The underlined `library` states the context of this invariant. The invariant states that the set of loans of books borrowed by cardholders is the same as the set of book copies checked out.

```
library
self.holdings.copy = self.cardholders.checkedout.borrowed
```

The preceding invariant is correct type-wise, but it is not true. The expression `self.holdings.copy` evaluates to the set of all instances of `copy` of book in the `library`. The other expression evaluates to the set of all instances of `copy` of book that are currently checked out. This would only be true if all the books in the `library` were currently checked out.

14.3.3 ATTRIBUTES

The expression can also refer to the value of an attribute. The same dot notation is used.

EXAMPLE 14.3
Write an invariant that says that "Grapes of Wrath" is not in the library.

```
book
self.name <> ''Grapes of Wrath''
```

The context is the class book. The expression `self.name` evaluates to the value of the name of the book.

14.3.4   PREDEFINED OPERATIONS

OCL has many operations on collections: size, count(object), includes (object), sum, and includesall(collection).

EXAMPLE 14.4
Write an invariant that says that no patron can have more than 10 books checked out at a time.

Patron
self.checkedout->size < 10

The expression self.checkedout evaluates to the set of loans associated with a patron. The operation size returns the number, and the invariant requires the number to be less than 10.

14.3.5   PRE- AND POST-CONDITIONS

In OCL, the context of the pre- and post-conditions must be shown as an underlined function. The syntax pre: and post distinguishes the pre- and post-condition. The keyword result can be used to designate the result of the operation.

The syntax @pre is used in OCL to specify the value before an operation.

EXAMPLE 14.5
Write pre- and post-conditions to ensure that a patron cannot check out more than 9 books.

patron::borrow
pre: self.checkedout->size < 9
post: self.checkedout->size < 10

or

post: self.checkedout@pre->size + 1 = self.checkedout->size

Review Questions

1. What kind of questions are specifications supposed to be able to answer?
2. Why would ambiguity be a problem?

3. Why are mathematical notions, such as sets, a good foundation for specifications?

4. What is the difference between preconditions, post-conditions, and invariants?

Problems

1. Given the object model shown in Fig. 14-2, evaluate each of the given OCL statements. If the statement is wrong, explain what is wrong and determine the simplest correction.

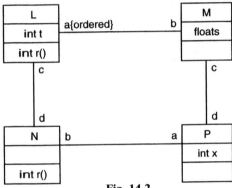

Fig. 14-2

L
```
self.c->size = 10
self.a = self.c.b.d
```

```
            L::r()  : int
pre: self.a.b = self.c.a
post: t = t@pre + 1
post: result = self.a->first.s
```

P
```
self.a.d->size > max
self.a.b = self.d.c
            N::q()  : int
pre: self.b->isEmpty
pre: self.d->forall( l |l.t < 10)
post: result = self.d->size
```

2. Given the object model shown in Fig. 14-3, explain each OCL statement. What does it specify? Is the OCL invariant reasonable? Is it always true?

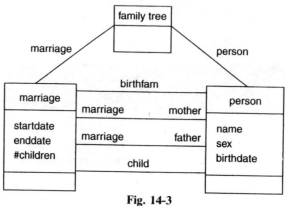

Fig. 14-3

<u>familytree</u>
   a) self.person = self.marriage.child

<u>marriage</u>
   b) self.child.birthfam = self
   c) self.husband.birthdate < self.wife.birthdate

<u>person</u>
   d) self.birthfam.child_include(self)
   e) self.marriage->size = 1
   f) self.marriage.wife.birthdate < self.birthdate

3. Write OCL constraints for a restaurant without a smoking section that seats customers in order of arrival.

```
Class group
    Char* name
    Int number
    Int arrivalorder
Class waitlist
    Group* list[MAX]
    Int listptr
    Void addtolist(group* newgroup)
    Group* seatnext()
Class restaurant
    Waitlist* waiting
    Void arrive(group* newgroup)
    Group* seat()
```

Answers to Review Questions

1. What kind of questions are specifications supposed to be able to answer?

Usually, the questions are about the behavior of the proposed software. Developers should be able to use the specifications to determine exactly what the software should do in a specified situation.

2. Why would ambiguity be a problem?

If the ambiguity means that the developer will interpret the specification differently than what the user wants, then there will be a problem.

3. Why are mathematical notions, such as sets, a good foundation for specifications?

Mathematical notions such as sets are a good foundation for specifications because sets and set operations are precisely defined. For example, the union of two sets is well understood. If the behavior of a function can be defined as operations on specified sets, then it will be easy to determine exactly what the function is supposed to do.

4. What is the difference between preconditions, post-conditions, and invariants?

A precondition is something that has to be true before a function can execute. A post-condition is something that has to be true on completion of the function. An invariant is something that should be true throughout the execution of the function. Actually, most invariants are true between every operation.

Answers to Problems

1. All are okay except for `pre:self.a.b = self.c.a`, which should be `pre: self.a.b = self.c.d`.

2. Given the object model shown in Fig. 14-4, explain each OCL statement. What does it specify? Is the OCL invariant reasonable? Is it always true?

```
familytree
    a) self.person = self.marriage.child

marriage
    b) self.child.birthfam = self
    c) self.husband.birthdate < self.wife.birthdate
```

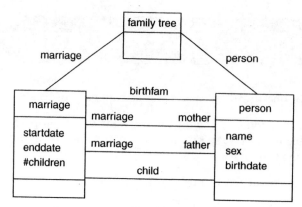

Fig. 14-4

<u>person</u>
d) self.birthfam.child_include(self)
e) self.marriage->size = 1
f) self.marriage.wife.birthdate < self.birthdate

a. This invariant says that the set of persons is the same as the set of all children or every person has his or her birth marriage listed. This is a reasonable invariant, and it is true if the data is complete.

b. This invariant says that every child has his or her birth family listed and it matches the instance that points to the person as a child. This is reasonable and is always true.

c. This says that every husband is older than his wife. This invariant can be stated, but it does not match reality.

d. This states that the set of children (siblings) reachable from the birthfam includes the person. This is reasonable and is always true.

e. This states that the set of marriages for a person is only one. It does not match reality.

f. Either your own birthday (if female) or your spouse's (if male) is less than yours. Not reasonable. Not always true.

3. Write OCL constraints for a restaurant without a smoking section that seats customers in order of arrival.

```
Class group
    Char* name
    Int number
    Int arrivalorder

Class waitlist
    Group* list[MAX]
    Int listptr
    Void addtolist(group* newgroup)
    Group* seatnext()
```

```
Class restaurant
  Waitlist* waiting
  Void arrive(group* newgroup)
  Group* seat()
```

Waitlist

```
    Self.Listptr = self.list->size
Void waitlist::addtolist(group* newgroup)
    Pre:   self.listptr < MAX
    Post: forall(i | list[i] = list[i-1]@pre)
          List[0] = newgroup
          Listptr = listptr@pre+1
Group* waitlist::seatnext()
    Pre:   self.listprt > 0
    Post: Result = list[listptr@pre]
          Self.listptr = self.listprt@pre - 1
Group* Restaurant::seat
    Pre:   waiting.waitlist->size > 0
    Post: waiting.waitlist->size = waiting. waitlist@pre->size
    - 1
      Result = waiting.seatnext()
      and forall (x : group | waiting.seatnext().arrivalorder
      <= x.arrivalorder)
```

INDEX